BROOKLANDS COLLEGE LIBRARY
HEATH ROAD, WEYBRIDGE, SURREY KT13 8TT
Tel: (01932) 797906

This item must be returned on or before the last date entered below. Subject to certain conditions, the loan period may be extended upon application to the Librarian

DATE OF RETURN	DATE OF RETURN	DATE OF RETURN

AUTHOR ___ GASKELL

TITLE Make your own Hollywood movie

CLASSIFICATION NO. ___ 778·5

ACCESSION NO. ___ 093161

MAKE YOUR OWN HOLLYWOOD MOVIE

A STEP-BY-STEP GUIDE TO SCRIPTING, STORYBOARDING,
CASTING, SHOOTING, EDITING AND PUBLISHING YOUR
VERY OWN BLOCKBUSTER MOVIE / ED GASKELL
ADDITIONAL PROJECTS / CHRIS KENWORTHY

ILEX

Make Your Own Hollywood Movie

First published in the United Kingdom in 2004 by
ILEX
The Old Candlemakers,
West Street,
Lewes,
East Sussex,
BN7 2NZ
www.ilex-press.com

This book was conceived by
ILEX, Cambridge, England

Publisher: Alastair Campbell
Executive Publisher: Sophie Collins
Creative Director: Peter Bridgewater
Editorial Director: Steve Luck
Editor: Stuart Andrews
Design Manager: Tony Seddon
Designer: Peter Burt
Artwork Assistant: Joanna Clinch
Development Art Director: Graham Davis
Technical Art Editor: Nicholas Rowland

British Library Cataloguing-in-Publication Data
A catalogue record for this book is available from
the British Library

ISBN 1-904705-31-6

Printed and bound in China

For more on making Hollywood movies visit:
www.holluk.web-linked.com

Contents

Introduction   6

1 The Digital Movie Studio   10

Digital Video   12
The Camera   14
Life Through a Lens   16
Features and Effects   18
Necessary Accessories   20
The Computer   22
Editing Hardware   24
Editing Software   26
Soft Options   28

2 Preproduction   30

Introduction   32
Hatching your Plot   34
Writing the Screenplay   36
Genre and Drama   38
Moving the Plot Along   40
Drawing on Ideas   44
Location, Location, Location   46
Setting Scenes   48
Stars and Actors   50
Finding the Crew   52
Art Department   54

3 The Shoot   56

Introduction   58
Hot Shots   60
Framing the Shot   62
Moving Pictures   64

Taking Control   66
Lighting   68
More on Light   70
Sound Advice   72
Shooting Dialogue   74
Louder Than Words   76
Cut and Cover   78

4 The Final Cut   80

Introduction   82
Importing the Footage   84
The Fourth Dimension   86
Cutting the Movie   88
Transitions   90
Movie Language and
    Timeline Tricks   94
Movie Magic   98
Colour Correction   102
Working with Titles   106

5 Editing Audio   110

Introduction   112
Controlling Volume   114
Talking Pictures   116
Audio Filters   118
Original Soundtracks   120
Dubbing Audio   122
Mixing and Panning   124

6 Distribution   126

Introduction   128
Make Your Own DVDs   130
Online Movies   134

7 Hollywood Tricks   136

Introduction   138
How to Make a Bluescreen   140
How to Use Chromakey   142
How to Use Smoke   144
How to Shoot Underwater   146
How to Create Gunshots   148
How to Fake Wounds   150
How to Shoot a Fight Scene   152
How to Shoot a Car Chase   154
How to Shoot Flashbacks   156
How to Create a Clone   158
How to Create a Trombone
    Shot   160
How to Shoot Reflections   162
How to Create a Ghost   164
How to Create a Werewolf   166
How to Create Small and
    Tall People   168
How to Create Rain   170
How to Recreate Absent Props   172
How to Shoot Day for Night   174
How to Build Lunar Landscapes   176
How to Create Space and Stars   178
How to Shoot Miniatures   180
How to Create an Explosion   182

Glossary   184
Index   188
Acknowledgements   192

Introduction

So here's the deal: you're not going to make a Hollywood movie

Even in la-di-da land where a mere 5 per cent of scripts get commissioned, only 1 per cent get green-lit. Sticking with percentage improbability, if you're in that 1 per cent, then trying to sell yourself as director – or having the slightest bit of control over the production – pushes the odds down to virtually zero.

So instead, you're going to make your own Hollywood movie.

Ownership is the greatest thing about digital video. You can own a digital video camera, a computer, and a bit of edit software for under £1000. And if gear is cheap, ideas are free. Owning the hardware and software costs cash, but owning the rights to your ideas, your scripts and your production costs nothing. It's yours – and nobody can take that away from you.

The cloud to this silver lining is that this killer combination of cheap gear and cheaper ideas makes nearly everybody in the world a potential director. If 80 per cent of students want to work in the media, then as many as 50 per cent might want to make movies (a hefty proportion of the rest aiming for the giddy heights of TV presenting). If one-quarter of the world's population is in primary, secondary and further education, then one eighth of the world could be gunning to make the next *Matrix*, *Blair Witch Project* or *Citizen Kane*. That's around eight hundred million budding shooters.

Coupled with this is the deception of glamour. Movies, Hollywood – two words that inspire an image which is absolutely not the reality. If only 12 per cent of the population are potential directors, then everyone's a critic. Hollywood is not a fashion show – it's a business that relies on product confidence for enough private and public investment to turn a profit. For those movies that do get made, how many run for two weeks and disappear? How many go straight to video, straight to television or are shelved forever when a company goes under or for political or litigious reasons? It happens to the best directors, so as sure as turkeys are turkeys, it can happen to you.

Daniel Myrick and Eduardo Sanchez found it incredibly difficult to strike the right deal that would enable a second movie after *The Blair Witch Project* because of a legacy of legal wranglings; Paul Verhoeven still has problems in LA after *Showgirls*, even though he's made money with every other production. At least Terry Gilliam managed to salvage a reasonably successful documentary out of his half-finished *Don Quixote* project.

Statistical deflation is the only way to control the inevitable disappointment of anticipation. And this is just part of it. Don't think your production (if you finish it) will be a release in the cinemas or for your creative psyche. If it's yours, you'll probably never be totally happy with it anyway. Expect the worst, expect an anticlimax: the best thing is to expect a lot of relief, not a major release.

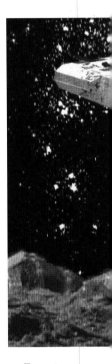

Still not put off?

Well, your chances of backyard success just doubled.

The start of any movie is the end – not just in script terms, which will be discussed later – but in respect of your aims and ambitions. The first question is whether or not you are intending to make money out of it. If you

While you might not have the budget to make your own *Star Wars* saga, you can still have a lot of fun trying. George Lucas may have abandoned his models for a CGI toybox, but that doesn't mean you have to do the same. With a simple bluescreen, some makeshift models and a little know-how, you can stage starship battles with the best of them.

are, the conditions under which you're shooting change entirely. This is the serious big boys' game. From contracts, budgets and shooting schedules via technical constraints and conventions to copyrights, marketing and distribution, the entire production is spent battling the administrative against the creative. In fact, it's a big girls' game as well. While the male megalomaniacs haven't been abandoned by Hollywood, women are becoming more and more successful in producer roles.

This book is not for those who have sold their houses to make a movie to make their career. This book is for those with a digital video camera, a computer, some cheap edit software, a group of friends, a bit of time, a bit of cash and a few ideas rattling around. If you are serious about trying to make it Big Time, then there's certainly no harm done by simply making your own production and using it as leverage. And as a template, Hollywood is not just the most famous, but the most challenging: with a product so expensive and so celebrated, will you be able to emulate it at home?

It's important to remember that you're not trying to copy an original; you're going to use the conventions, language and effects of a Hollywood movie as a tool to work through your own ideas. The Hollywood template is simply the biggest theme park in the movie universe. Your mind is the playground and your movie will hopefully be the best ride.

When you're building that ride, don't allow your ideas to be confined to what you can physically represent on video. We'll give you some ideas to push past those limitations towards the end of the book. Find some balance between shying away from showing the impossible, and being conceptually overambitious as to what you can do. It's all a question of production values.

Production values will be a major factor in the quality of your movie, and they will be limited by your budget. If you want your production values to exceed your production costs, you'll need forethought, focus and imagination. The decisions you make will affect what you get on screen. If a beach location is going to take a day out of your schedule, are you going to sacrifice two standard interior dialogue scenes and cover the holes left in your plot elsewhere? If you want to grade your entire movie, are you going to lose the manufacture of your monster so that you can afford some better software? It's up to you, and you had better get it right.

But it's not just production values that make a better movie. What made *The Blair Witch Project* a more successful movie than *Godzilla*? Working around the limitations of the budget helps, but it's the story that makes all the difference. Get it working in balance with the medium, the budget and the style, and you could have a backroom blockbuster on your hands.

The one factor that both of these movies had in common was the marketing push. Faced with the closed shop of Hollywood, a clever internet campaign and word of mouth speak volumes over an intensive, expensive cynical campaign. Whereas *The Blair Witch Project*'s trump card was 'Truth', *Godzilla*'s ('Size Does Matter') was patently cynical. Really, story matters more.

The digital revolution impacted first with those who could afford it (read Hollywood). Using computers to turn fragile, physical film stock into digital data made absolute sense. Suddenly, there was no degeneration of quality – clips and edits could be stored minutely and backed-up safely, effects could be more elaborate and editing could be quicker and more precise.

When the revolution hit the amateur scene, however, its effects became even more pervasive. Whereas Hollywood has kept digital (mostly) in postproduction, the low-budget and no-budget crowd realized it could exploit the benefits throughout the production cycle. Certainly, there's one thing that software and hardware manufacturers focus on when designing their gear. With a potential eight hundred million customers, they're building products that can really help you make your own Hollywood movie.

You don't need a room full of hardware to make your own Hollywood movie. With an Apple PowerBook, a DV camera and a copy of Final Cut Pro, you're not a million miles away from a professional setup. Buy the gear and all you need is the creativity.

Okay, so there's this movie you once saw, right? And it made you want to become a director? While you might feel you're paying homage to *Reservoir Dogs*, your audience might just feel it's a no-brain parody. If you're going to make something, you really might as well make it with your own ideas, from your own perspective.

The best way to start making a movie is to look at the end. Is it worth your time and money? And if so, how are you going to spend both of them? Think about your final product, where your audience is and how you're going to market and distribute it. When you're already the producer and director, it's likely that the rest will be in your job description too.

If you think you know who your friends are... you're wrong. Dead wrong.

Raising your production values means taking a little more effort in getting your shots. You don't have to limit yourself to your shoot dates. If you've got a DV camera and you see something in nature, that'll give your movie three seconds of extra gloss - get out, get your actor and then get your shot.

the digital movie studio

Digital Video

This book is concerned with how to recreate Hollywood using digital methods. But don't think that Hollywood doesn't use digital technology. It does – and increasingly.

Since the early days, Hollywood's production cycle has been locked into 35mm film. That is to say that a movie, in its physical form, comes in vertically-running reels of still photographs, 35mm wide with audio tracks running simultaneously along the side of each frame. Each image is created by an amount of light travelling through a lens to hit a negative rolling behind the shutter. The negative is processed with chemicals that polarize the negative to a positive image, and a cutting print is born. From here, the movie is edited by physically cutting and splicing the print.

This is not a digital process – it's an optical process and an analogue one. Our experience of the real world is also analogue – it's based on our ability to process a mass of sensory data from each of our five senses. Time-based media (movie, video, television and so on) use just two of these senses: hearing and seeing. The audio and the visual are combined with time to create an experience that resembles our experience of the real world. Each individual shot within a film or video represents the analogue world in real time. Any edit to the shot is a manipulation of time, and time can be contracted (fast motion or cutting frames out) or protracted (slow

motion or putting other shots in) as the filmmaker desires.

Your Hollywood movie won't be shot on film, but on digital video. Light will come through the lens of a DV camera and be converted by a CCD sensor into a stream of digital information. That data will be compressed and manipulated, then decompressed and interpreted for playback at a later date.

Why is this difference important? It's important because traditional psychology says that a movie isn't a movie unless it's shot on film and over ninety minutes long. Luckily, while the traditional minimum

length still exists, the second convention is being overturned. The digital 'look' is now becoming more acceptable in Hollywood.

The 'look' defines the vital difference between analogue film and digital video, and it's defined by the difference between the way that each handles their images.

Film running at speed through the camera does so at 24 frames every second. Even to the naked eye, this appears slightly animated with quick movement. It is. Within the seamless world of analogue, film is only taking those 24 still frames out of the infinite information that the eye captures like a flickerbook. Video on the other hand – whether analogue or digital – doesn't capture frames. It samples light and colour and shuffles the information onto magnetic tape. There is no physical animation involved to deceive the eye. Instead, video samples the image either 25 times a second or 29.97 times a second. This difference is an international discrepancy. The former is PAL (Phase Alternation Line), the main European standard, and the latter is NTSC (National Television Standards Committee) for North America and Japan.

While 25 and 29.97 don't sound so far from 24 frames a second, video's technique of sampling takes two 'fields' for each 'frame'. In short, it's sampling an image 50 or 60 times a second. This is what gives digital video its life-like quality and seamless movement – but because of the medium's eagerness to feed off available light, depth of field is automatically lost, resulting in a flattening of the image.

This 'look' of reality is entirely different from the richly contrived imitation of life that traditional film has given us over the history of Hollywood. Our eyes can notice the slight animation – the unreality – of movies and we're subconsciously comfortable knowing that this is a staged movie. Digital video has given filmmakers an opportunity to play upon this knowledge to stage movies within a supposed reality. It's a leg up over any Hollywood method of making us believe in their filmed movie, hence *The Blair Witch Project* – a distinctly guerrilla affair.

The success of *The Blair Witch Project, Timecode (2000), Baise-moi, Dancer in the Dark, The Idiots,* and other 'dogme' work has done all the hard work for you. Hollywood loves to hijack a success story, embrace it and call it its own, which has made the low-budget digital movie a serious commercial possibility.

Necessity used to be the mother of invention, but how quickly things change. These early theatrically-distributed digital video movies have helped to transform the medium from a budget-driven necessity (*The Last Broadcast*'s home video documentary, *My Little Eye*'s CCTV monitoring) to a valid style choice (though one that's still often budget-driven). A modern audience is quite happy to accept the digital video of *28 Days Later*—and while the style seems gritty and edgy, they're still watching a traditionally-told Hollywood movie. What's more, innovative directors are now utilizing all that video has to offer.

The tradition with televised video is one of quick shoots, long takes, few cuts and uninvolving shots. But the new Hollywood video success story has shaken up broadcast TV to make it more dynamic and visually challenging. You can take elements of this style and use it if you want. If you don't, the digital video look isn't your only option. With £3000 to spend, there are 24-frames-a-second DV cameras with 'film-like' colour qualities for those who want to have their cake (cheapness and immediacy) and eat it too (the 'look' of film). Whether you're a budding Lars von Trier or a wannabe David Lean, it's an exciting time to be wielding a digital video camera.

The difference between the look of video and that of film is one of chrominance, luminance, depth and movement. There's an intangible richness to film that makes it look expensive and classy when the two are compared. This historical pre-programming of an audience is the first hurdle to be jumped when your movie hits the screen.

14 The Camera

Like film, the digital process is based on the amount of light entering the camera lens – and that's where the similarity ends. Instead of the light hitting photosensitive frames, it hits a Charge Coupled Device (CCD). The device is a wafer-thin screen made from thousands or even millions of semi-conductors, which each turn the amount of light that they're receiving from that part of the image into a small electrical signal. This pulse's strength is relative to the amount of chrominance (colour) and luminance (light) for each pixel.

The resolution of the image is based on the amount of semiconductors available to produce the picture. To that purpose, the more pixels, the better the resolution, and the crisper and more detailed the image will be.

The older analogue video cameras took the information in from the CCD as a direct copy of how light and colour fell within the frame. In the real world, there is an infinite variation in light and colour, and that is what is captured. Analogue video cameras recorded the real world onto magnetic tape as the same infinite values, represented as well as possible by electromagnetic pulses. Digital video, on the other hand, has only a certain amount of maximum 10-bit variations (256 different values for luminance; 1.1 billion for chrominance) to capture the same information. So why should a digital picture be better than an analogue one? The short answer is that it sometimes isn't, but often is. The long answer is by understanding how the compression (encoding) of the light works in order to store it as digital data.

While the cheaper and more compact digital video cameras have just one CCD with as many pixels as they can jam into it, semi-professional and professional cameras have three – one for each primary colour. The red (R), green (G) and blue (B) CCDs still do the same basic job, but with more dedication to a truer colour.

The more money you pay, the more pixels you get. Digital video pixels are rectangular, to work with the eventual ratio of playout. Whether PAL or NTSC, standard definition is 4:3 – the ratio of a standard television. High Definition Television (HDTV), the next industry broadcast standard, is fundamentally true 16:9 widescreen. This, of course, is far more useful to anyone trying to emulate Hollywood, purely because it is one of the many cinematic ratios, unlike 4:3.

High Definition is currently the preserve of expensive professional cameras; 16:9 widescreen shooting is not. A number of inexpensive DV cameras now offer a widescreen mode – the only thing you need to watch out for is whether it's true widescreen and not a cheap simulation: some models just put black bars over the top and bottom of your image, cutting down the resolution available for the actual movie; others stretch the image out for a weird, distorted look. Try before you buy.

Up to this point on the CCD, the information that represents the picture as an electrical signal is still analogue. The next step is for each pixel to undergo translation to digital. This task is performed by an analogue-to-digital converter (ADC), which takes the extent of each pixel's electronic pulse and gives it a value based on a series of 0s and 1s (0 for digital is off, and 1 is on). For each pixel, the value combines luminance and chrominance.

Because of the infinite values of analogue light and colour, values have to be sampled, recalculated with algorithms and then compressed to fit into digital's limited range of values. Compression is the one factor that makes digital a joy in terms of speed, but a potential nightmare in terms of image fidelity – but all good and bad things come to those who wait…

It's not until the information is shuffled and spewed out onto the tape or into the hard drive, that it can then be reread as digital information. Viewing the images, however, is not the same as viewing a digitized image. Instead, what you are seeing is a digitally compressed analogue image being retranslated back to a version of the analogue image that once hit the CCD. Viewing this image isn't possible unless the camera, the hard drive or whatever source you're playing your digital images on, can reconvert the digital using a DAC – a digital-to-analogue converter.

There are a few different types of digital video camera available to you, and these have a few different ways of recording data. Most consumer DV cameras use the MiniDV tape standard; a few use the smaller MicroMV or larger Digital8 standards, or even recordable DVD. What you have to remember in all of this is that digital is digital is digital, just as a 0 is a 0 and a 1 is a 1. Of course, the graduation in price in this table indicates the quality of the video. It's true that 3 CCDs give you more reliable colour and more pixels give you clearer definition, but a good lens, some manual controls and a few audio connections are the only essentials. MPEG-4 recording, high-resolution stills capture, memory card support and a huge LCD screen are all very nice, but they won't actually help you to make your own Hollywood movie. Don't be blinded by the manufacturers' jargon.

The bottom line for buying a DV camera is to see and try as many as you can in your price range, and to check reviews in the specialist press and online. That way, you'll get the right tool for the job.

Sony's DCR-HC85 features a two-megapixel 16:9 CCD, a 10x Carl Zeiss zoom lens and a manual focus ring: all excellent features for moviemaking.

A good budget model, such as Canon's MV700i, can still produce high-quality results if funds are tight. Its features include an 18x optical zoom.

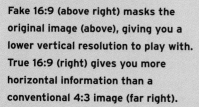

Fake 16:9 (above right) masks the original image (above), giving you a lower vertical resolution to play with. True 16:9 (right) gives you more horizontal information than a conventional 4:3 image (far right).

16 Life Through a Lens

Cinematography is all about control. The great DP (Director of Photography) knows exactly what combination of lens, lighting and exposure will get the effect he or she is looking for.

That's the Hollywod theory. What you'll find in practice is that all this will happen without you having to do anything. All digital video cameras are automatic. Your job is to control the image and get the best out of it with the camera.

But there are reasons to go beyond the automatic settings. Taking more control of your image releases you from the terrifying grasp of 'Funniest Home Videos'. Assuming that you're not making your movie with spontaneous skateboarding aardvarks, control will help you get your creative intentions on screen. For this reason, you need a camera that can get you out of automatic mode. At the very least, you need controls for exposure, shutter speed and focus.

If you are buying a camera, those are the factors that should persuade you, and not in-camera effects or length of digital zoom – both of which you'll probably find useless. The lens is the most important part of any camera, and on-line resources are very good at providing informative sounding boards for whinging or glorifying users.

Before you start taking or rejecting their advice, though, here come the all-things-Hollywood that you'll need your camera to do.

The lens is your gateway to pictures, and it's light that makes them. Having a lens that feeds that light in truly and correctly is vital. MiniDV cameras are tailored to be compact. For this reason, the lenses are designed to let in as much light as possible. To do so, the lens is designed to be slightly wide-angled. The drawback of this is that such lenses are subject to refraction – creating sunspots on the image.

There are plenty of different lenses, lens converters, and filters on the market, and they're made by nearly every DV camera manufacturer. The biggest difference between lenses is how the glass is constructed to focus rays of light. While a wide-angled lens pours in more light from a wider vision and creates an extended depth of field, a telephoto lens narrows this angle and increases the depth of field.

The zoom function on your DV camera is best left alone. Not only does any camera movement become grossly exaggerated, but the image doesn't stand up to scrutiny. If the warnings don't work, try an image for size. This is a digital zoom at 120x: the blown-up pixels turn the picture into nothing more than a hideous mess.

A lens converter is a device that can be fitted between the body of the camera and the lens in order to increase the focal length. An increase in focal length reduces the depth of field and allows a subject and the background to be separated. Doing so will also give you enough room to pull–focus or rack–focus.

Perhaps sticking with an optical zoom takes your fancy? Here, a slight colour saturation brings out the true nature of how the camera is dealing with the pixels. It's not a good look.

18 Features and Effects

Just as the lens is the most important weapon to get your Hollywood pictures, your built-in camera effects are probably the least essential. As you might have noticed while watching your favourite movie, there are few instances of trails and polarization used. It's not that in-camera effects can't be used – in fact, Marc Evans used night vision incredibly effectively in *My Little Eye* – it's just that they need to be used carefully and creatively.

EFFECTS

There are two types of effects available for digital video cameras – picture effects and digital effects. They're actually both digital, and in both cases your data is being processed and altered. While picture effects act like painting effects, changing the look of the movie during every frame in which they're used, digital effects apply themselves to the shot over time.

In either case, there's one good reason not to use them: because filters change the values of the digital data that makes up your movie, you can't just remove them later. If you shoot with an in-camera effect you're stuck with it forever, so unless you know what you're doing, you should always shoot clean. You'll still be able to get the same effect – and a more controllable one – in the edit.

One possible exception is the trail. If you want to make a shot a little more dynamic than it actually is, a trail leaves an echo of the action for a given number of frames on the same frame. Its use may also extend to dream sequences if required.

ZOOMS

The next thing to avoid is the zoom – after all, Hollywood doesn't use it. Pushes are slight nudges with the camera lens towards a subject, and are perhaps the closest thing. Occasionally, a zoom can be used to fantastic effect because it is unexpected. The hospital shock in *Exorcist III* is one of the few successful examples, but in most cases, using the zoom pinpoints your movie as an amateur effort.

A more common use of the zoom is its reverse – the pull-out (as

shown along the bottom of the page). This works by putting a subject in a location, and usually indicates their isolation. This example, used with a welling choral soundtrack, tells an audience that the victim is alone, and that she's going to have to fight for her life.

IMAGE STABILIZERS

Once you've played with effects and realized that most of them are useless, there are the more practical features of a camera to consider – image stabilizers are one. Image stabilizers are common on all MiniDV and MicroMV cameras, but operate in different ways, depending upon the manufacturer. While Electronic Image Stabilizers (EIS) compensate for any shake or jerk with a mathematical compensation of pixels, Optical Image Stabilizers surreptitiously shoot slightly wider and compensate using gyros and mechanics. This can be responsible for not quite giving you the end shot that you want if you're making a quick move. Electrical Image Stabilizers, though, in rearranging

pixels, can sometimes get it wrong, leading to artefacts – visible blocks that turn up to ruin your picture.

BATTERIES

Shooting can be an unpredictably long process. This – coupled with human error (switching cameras off Standby) – highlights the need for a longer-lasting battery. There are two sides to every story, though, and ways that battery time can be saved. Flip-out screens sap a whole load of energy, as will overusing the zoom.

BATTERY TYPE

Different battery types won't dictate which camera you buy, but you should know something about them. With MiniDV and MicroMV, the chances are that your batteries are either Lithium Ion (Li-Ion) or Nickel Metal Hydride (NiMH). The latter is the technology of choice, as it makes for smaller, lighter and longer-lasting batteries.

Sony has another little trick up its sleeves. Its infoLITHIUM batteries carry information to the camera itself, such as how long until total discharge – but they're fundamentally Li-Ion batteries in not-so-cheap clothing. Whichever battery you use, you should always have a second charged, preferably one with a few hours' capacity. It might weigh more and cost more, but a heavier, expensive battery might just save you a reshoot.

DV cameras are often sold with low-life batteries, so it makes sense to buy a longer-lasting back-up to take with you on location. Get both batteries recharged before you go out on a shoot, and keep your charger handy if you're close to a power source during filming.

SPEC LIST

→ **included camera battery**
→ **extended-life camera battery**

Necessary Accessories

The great thing about DV is that there are so many extra toys and gadgets available. Partly because it's such a growth industry, more and more peripherals are being tailor-made for smaller crews, smaller budgets and smaller cameras. Not all are truly essential.

Whatever your production might be, and however small your budget, you can help to raise your production values by investing in a few useful accessories.

TRIPODS

If you're a true auteur, tripods can be one of those things that you'll kick against. They never smack of kinetic cinema and instead appear fussy and old-school. Okay, but get ready to kick yourself on location when you haven't got one.

The point about tripods is that they help provide the texture for your finished movie. No matter how dynamic and improvised you want your movie to look, there is no handheld camera in the world that gives the same, sharp, smooth image as a controlled shot from a firmly placed tripod.

Apart from adding stability to the shot, tripods have three other uses. First, you can 'lock-off' the camera, securing it so it doesn't move. Second and third, it allows you to pan (a smooth movement on a horizontal pivot) and tilt (the same, but vertical). Either one looks better if done with the aid of a tripod.

Tripods for DV are sold for the digital video market, but double for use with telescopes. That doesn't mean to say the price has to be astronomical, but there's no point in cutting corners. A tripod is there to be stable and reliable, and the less cash that you fork out, the more flimsy your product is liable to be. DV and MiniDV tripods indicate a maximum weight (total your camera with the heaviest battery to get this). The heavier the weight on the head, the smoother any pans or tilts are likely to be. Weight on the head, though, can make a tripod unstable on the legs, so make sure there's a wide enough spread on them.

Quick release plates are always a good idea, as they make setting up and breaking down the shoot that much faster. This means that the screwhole in the bottom of your camera is already threaded to a plate, which simply clicks into the panhead of the tripod.

A fluid action is essential – but if you've got a heavy camera and battery, make sure the clamps can hold the weight. Ideally, you want a claw ball leveller for versatility of angle, and a stud to cover vibration from the legs up to the head.

MICS

Audio, audio, audio: the three things that are easily forgotten when shooting. Spending a bit of money not only helps you to get it right in the shoot, but the hole in your pocket might make you remember. Hollywood movies are driven by dialogue because it's the easiest way to tell a story, but it's useless when your actors' mouths are open and all you can hear is a passing bus. Getting away from using the camera mic is certainly important when it comes to quiet scenes. No matter what you might be monitoring in headphones, servo sounds can become quite apparent in some cameras during playback.

Camera mics are cardioid condensers. This means that their receptive area is in a heart shape from a point at the back of the handle and swelling to slightly left and right of the mic head. A condenser mic is one that has a light, thin diaphragm – it's sensitive and can pick a lot up, which can be a dream in some situations and, yes, a nightmare in others.

The problem with camera mics is that they're too good – they pick everything up, whether you want it or not. Just as using manual settings and a tripod will give you control over your shots, so a plug-in mic will allow control over your audio. An external mic becomes very useful when used in tandem with the camera mic. In the camera's menu, you should be able to turn the mic off completely or adjust the levels to give two audio sources.

Audio patterns come in a variety of cardioid shapes, as well as bi-directional (polar opposite left and right pickup – good for interviews) and omnidirectional (all directions – great for ambience). Think carefully about the kind of sound that you're seeking to capture.

For dialogue in the field, forget the cheaper radio mics. Using VHF radio frequencies to channel your actors' vocal expertise on location becomes more of an interference minefield. A couple of good UHF lavaliers (or lavs for short) are the best thing to have on hand. Lavs can either be wired straight into your camera's mic port, or used wireless with a transmitter and receiver.

A lavalier consists of a transmitter and receiver, both of which run with domestic batteries. It's always better to use cable than to go wireless if at all possible, and a discreetly lapelled lav will let you run straight into your DV Cam's mic port with a minijack.

SPEC LIST

→ **mini-DV tripod**
→ **external cardioid microphone**
→ **lavalier microphone**

The Computer

If the mantra says 'think to the edit', then your computer and the software that you have – or that you're going to get – is something which will always be your ultimate be-all and end-all. It's got to be right: the right level, the right price and the right tool for the job.

There are two basic choices here: a PC or an Apple Mac. For simple Hollywood moviemaking, a Mac is a great all-in-one choice. Not only do all models come with iMovie as standard, but more confident users can upgrade to Final Cut Express or Final Cut Pro and use something that is industry standard. Also, there are no incompatibility problems with a Mac – unlike a PC.

PCs can be more problematic. While a Mac and its applications are governed by Apple, PCs have an open architecture – a free-for-all for all hard and software manufacturers. This means that there are no hard-and-fast rules or laws – and it's not unusual that some cards, plug-ins and applications simply don't recognize one another, let alone talk to each other. When they do work, though, PCs can work harder and faster for less money than a Mac.

Any computer is made up of three main elements: a CPU (Central Processing Unit), a motherboard and an HDD (Hard Disk Drive). The motherboard contains all the most important controller chips, and it's also where your processor – your CPU – is located. It's essential that the motherboard and processor

work in harmony. If you're using a Mac, that's a given. If you're using a PC, your CPU will either be in Intel's Pentium or AMD's Athlon series.

Both are continuously updated, but the more recent and speedy they are, the faster they will work in the heat of an edit. The speed is usually measured in GHz (gigahertz) or an equivalent rating, but bear in mind that differences in system technology mean that GHz ratings don't mean everything: a 3.2GHz Pentium 4 system won't actually be twice as fast as a 1.6GHz Power Mac G5. Also, some systems come in dual processor configurations, with the two processors sharing the burden of running your software. This will make a difference if you're using particular applications – Final Cut Pro, for instance – but in many basic editing packages it won't make any noticeable difference.

Beware: PCs tagged 'multi-media' aren't always as suitable as you might think – it can just mean that the system has a DVD drive and some means of Internet access. What you should look for is the specification of the computer, and whether it matches the recommended specification for the software you want to use.

Obviously, hard disk capacity is vital – you need a few gigabytes just for the operating system and applications. Worse, every four-and-a-half minutes of DV will gobble 1Gb of hard-disk space – and if you're making a Hollywood movie of ninety minutes, that's going to mean losing 20Gb without any consideration for your shooting ratio (the ratio of footage shot to footage used in the final movie).

Between the hard drive and the processor is your RAM (random access memory). This is a temporary storage area for all the information that your CPU is busy processing. While it's in this memory bank, your data can be easily accessed for a quicker response.

The speed of your machine in handling any edit software is dependent on its amount of RAM and the ability of your software to utilize RAM efficiently. Your editing software needs to create effects and transitions by making calculations on your video data, so it needs to have both the original data and the results of those calculations close to hand. The more RAM it has, the more capacity your computer has to do these complex tasks, and the more work it can do at one time. Most computers now use fast DDR SDRAM memory, and for video work it's wise to avoid systems that use the older SDRAM standard.

Of course, none of this is any good unless you can actually take your movies in and out, which makes the connections at the back of the machine essential. At the least, your Hollywood movie will

Apple's wallet-friendly iBook, iMac and eMac computers are perfect for digital moviemaking. With G4 processors and DDR SDRAM, they're fast enough for the job, they contain FireWire inputs as standard and Apple's excellent iMovie editing application comes bundled with the system. They look good, too.

The cable that you're most likely to need: a 6- to 4-pin FireWire. Data transfer is more reliable over shorter distances, though, and you don't want to work with anything over 9 metres (about 100cm) without a signal booster somewhere along the line.

The leading alternative to FireWire on PC is a USB2 connection. As it transfers data at higher speeds than standard FireWire, it's a genuine competitor. The downside is that – unlike FireWire – it relies on your computer to do the talking. If you want to hedge your bets and cover both bases, this IOGEAR USB2/FireWire Combo Card will slot into your PC and do precisely that.

involve getting your shots from DV and onto your computer, in which case you will need a DV input.

The standard DV input is IEEE 1394, more catchily known as 'FireWire' or 'i.Link'. It's all the same, but you will need two things: a FireWire cable which runs from the camera to the computer, and a FireWire connection on your computer. That one FireWire cable carries information both ways, copying the video signal not as a series of image frames, but as a stream of digital data.

There are two types of FireWire connection – 4-pin and 6-pin – the difference being that a 4-pin carries data only, while a 6-pin can also carry power (that is, the computer will power up the camera). MiniDV and MicroMV cameras tend to have 4 pins, mainly for size reasons, while the FireWire ports on desktop computers are almost always 6-pin.

FireWire ports are now included on most PCs and Macs, with the sockets built onto or connected to the motherboard. Alternatively, they might be included as part of a sound card or even a video capture card. These may contain additional inputs and outputs apart from Firewire, may include hardware to speed up special-effects, and might come bundled with editing software.

Why more inputs and outputs? Aside from digital data, you may want to use and import old analogue video. Analogue images may come from VHS or Hi-8 tapes, or any cine film that you might have duped onto analogue tapes. Despite their inferior quality, these can be worth using for a worn or old-fashioned effect.

If you have this sort of material and your system comes without a video capture card, you can still buy one separately, with instructions on how to slot it into your computer. That's why, when buying a PC, it's worth making sure that there are enough slots for any hardware you might want to add later.

WHAT YOU NEED IN YOUR EDITING SYSTEM

- Either a PC or Notebook running Windows XP Home or Windows XP Professional or an Apple iMac, iBook, eMac, PowerBook or Power Mac running Mac OS X
- Minimum 800MHz Processor
- Minimum 256Mb of DDR SDRAM
- Minimum 40Gb HDD
- 1 x FireWire in/out port or video capture card
- 1 x FireWire cable

Editing Hardware

The computer isn't the only essential item in your digital video-editing suite. Video data doesn't mean a thing until it hits the screen, which is why your monitor is so vitally important.

A monitor can either be CRT desktop (cathode ray tube) or a laptop's plasma/LCD (gaseous/liquid crystal display). The former uses anodes to focus and accelerate electron beams to individual red, green or blue phosphors coating the screen, which glow in combination (chrominance) and strength (luminance) to the signal. An LCD, on the other hand, is a fluorescent lightbox that polarizes light through liquid crystal transistors (pixels).

Okay, that's the science bit over...

The thing is, computer monitors differ quite a lot from the TV you will (probably) end up watching your movie on. Like many computer monitors, most televisions have a CRT screen. But, whereas the signal running from the computer to the monitor consists of separate red, green and blue signals, the signal running into a TV is a little more complicated. In many cases, the TV signal will be a composite, with the red, green and blue signals merged into one, resulting in a slight loss of colour quality and resolution. The signal between computer and screen is, in most cases, still analogue, so there will be some degradation, but not to the same extent. In fact, if

you use a flat panel display with a DVI (Digital Visual Interface) connection, wired up to a graphics card with the same, the signal stays digital all the way, meaning it will be brighter and clearer than it ever would be on TV.

Secondly, computer CRTs run at about one-third of the brightness of a TV screen, with more pixels (meaning the resolution is higher), and the screen updates using a method called progressive scan.

What does that mean? Well, scanning is the way that each field is refreshed on screen. If it's progressive, it means that images are refreshed line by line from the top to the bottom of the screen. Televisions tend to use interlaced scanning (although some expensive models can switch to progressive). This means that the electron beams deliver all the odd-numbered scan lines from top to bottom, and then come back to do the even-numbered scan lines. Because the phosphors used in CRTs glow for a time and then fade, the eye doesn't perceive the transition between the two different field scans.

The difference between computer-monitor and television CRTs is actually noticeable in this scanning process, and while progressive

scanning can be tiring on the eyes (it flickers), interlaced scanning tends to produce more 'jaggies' (aliasing issues) and artefacts (stray pixels), and results in an image that isn't usually so clear.

All of these issues add up to mean one thing: video, graphics and text that look fine on a computer screen may not look so fine on a TV. In other words, the image you see on your computer screen isn't always the final result.

Sound

Fidelity issues are not just confined to pictures. While your images are important, your audio is crucial. Dialogue in your Hollywood movie relies on being clear, levelled and balanced, and it needs to reflect how your characters are shot. Audio is one of those things that you don't notice if it's good, but the entire production becomes unwatchable if it's not. The only way of keeping track of this in the edit is with the combination of amp, speakers and sound card worthy of your efforts.

Like video capture cards, sound cards are sold separately, but the good news is that any PC you buy will have acceptable sound capabilities. Of course, a more

SPEC LIST

→ **1 x CRT/LCD monitor**

→ **1 x amp and 2 x speakers, or integrated speaker set**

→ **1 x sound card with up-to-date Windows drivers (PC only)**

While cables might seem mundane, and even outdated in this wireless age, getting complicated digital information from a computer output to a CRT input needs to be done quickly and without loss. If this is over a longer distance than a standard desktop computer to desktop monitor, only specialist cables such as this 3-metre Griffin ADC will do the job efficiently.

Hewlett Packard's Presario 8000 has two 120Gb hard drives, which is certainly enough to keep you going for a while. More and more desktop systems are moving towards LCD screens, but it's worth checking that the screen can cope with fast-moving video. On some cheaper displays, any fast movement results in a messy blur. You should be safe with big brand names, however.

Creative's SoundBlaster Audigy 2 sound card is often found within the casing of a standard computer. That doesn't mean, though, that it's a very standard bit of kit. Thanks to games and multi-media, PC users have become pretty demanding, and the audio capabilities of most PCs are up to the demands of moviemaking.

expensive sound card comes with extra features. They may have a better dynamic range if you want to import a separate audio track. They may have a better set of built-in instrument samples or synthesized sounds if you want to compose music for your movie. Or they might offer more effective sampling capabilities if you want to capture sound to add to your video at a later date. None of these things might sound that useful to you, but – as is so often the case – more money spent on the system from the start gives you more flexibility later on.

BURN, BABY, BURN

The final thing your computer needs is some means of getting your work off your computer and keeping it safe. Most PCs these days come with a recordable CD-RW drive, allowing you to copy files to a recordable CD or a rewritable CD (so called because you can write over it again and again). That's fine for audio files and still photographs, but the 700Mb capacity doesn't make much sense with huge video files. Luckily, recordable and rewritable DVD drives are tumbling in price to under £100, allowing you to store 4.7Gb (or 9Gb in some cases) on a single disk. There are some complications, in that there are two standards of recordable DVD – DVD-R and DVD+R – and three standards of rewritable DVD: DVD-RW, DVD+RW and DVD-RAM. This becomes important if you're planning to burn finished movies to DVD and play them back later on a conventional DVD player. While most players will play DVD-R disks, not all will play all three rewritable standards. If you want to take your finished masterpiece straight to your home DVD player, it's worth checking up beforehand.

Editing Software

You can't do anything with your moving images unless you've got some editing software to take them in and chop them around a bit. Editing your video isn't really that different from what you do when you process words on a computer – it's all cut-and-paste convenience and there's no reason at all to be scared. Everything's undoable, remakeable and salvageable, and you won't lose anything while you're doing it.

Editing software should allow you to do a few fundamental things. It will let you capture and import your clips, drag them onto your timeline, trim your clips' in and out points to the exact frame that you want and export your finished timeline as a movie file.

Beyond these essentials, you'll find your package a lot more suitable for movie work if you can join your clips with transitions (at least dissolves) and correct colour, contrast and brightness. It also helps if you can change the opacity of your clips, control their motion, work with mattes, control and mix audio, create titles and work to a widescreen aspect ratio.

In the basics, most good edit software does the same sort of thing, but each package might treat your footage in different ways. The most noticeable will be on the timeline. A timeline is where your clips will be put in chronological order. It's a comprehensive linear environment in a non-linear edit world. The lower end of editing software will just have

one line for your clips, one line for your transitions between clips and one line for audio. The more money spent, the greater the likelihood that you'll have multiple video and audio tracks, which gives you flexibility and enables you to layer clips on top of each other and create composite images. You don't have to spend much more to do this – and that versatility will be worth more to you than the cash.

A timeline that does have multiple video tracks often operates using A and B roll. If you come across this, it means that any transition takes place between clip A and clip B, allowing you to overlap your clips and tailor the transition to exactly the right frames between the two. It creates a chequerboard effect that is a more literal visualization of what is happening on your timeline.

When picking out your edit software, think about how you plan on distributing your final movie. If you're putting it online, you might want to export it as streaming media or as MPEG-2 to DVD – and it might

save you a few notes to find edit software that's capable of doing this without a separate encoder package. Encoding is the process of finalizing and compressing your video – taking your raw DV file and putting it in a format that's ready to share with the world at large.

Compression needs something called a codec, which stands for Compress/Decompress, and is the means by which your video data is shrunk for storage or expanded for viewing. Clips are compressed to make them take up less space, so they are easier for the computer to handle at speed. They are then decompressed when the clip or movie is played out from the computer. Not all compression formats or codecs are equal – some don't shrink the data so effectively, others shrink it by rounding the chrominance, luminance and resolution up or down at the expense of the overall image. Some can shrink the video down into tiny files without you losing anything noticeable. Expensive encoding or DVD authoring packages will have more options and better codecs. They might seem expensive, but you're forking out for brains. Just be aware that if your edit software came free with the computer, it may not have the best encoder and your picture may not fare well blown up at your local IMAX cinema.

The more complicated your edit (the more tracks, the more effects, the more clips, the more transitions), the more time your computer will need to process the information before you can actually view the

Pinnacle Systems used to monopolize the pre-installed, prepacked PC edit software market. Today, though, they've made enough of a mark to stand alone. This is MovieBox DV, one of their lower-end products. It's fundamentally a break-out box to allow the capture of digital and analogue images into your PC.

As always, such a big box hides a lot of air and a little software – in this case, Pinnacle's Studio 8. It's simple edit stuff that makes it easy for you, with timelines that look more like storyboards.

Sony's Vegas 4.0 is a more sophisticated – and therefore more expensive - affair. Never let a busy screen put you off, though. All of the elements shown above are accessible if you want to colour-correct and make your production ready for DVD or even broadcast, indicating just how serious a tool it is.

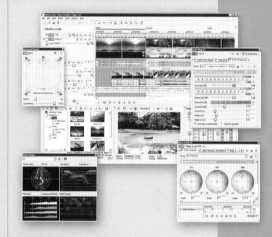

finished sequence. This is called rendering, and it's going to be the most tedious thing in your edit.

For this reason, increasing numbers of 'here's-one-I-made-earlier' special effects now come pre-installed in most good editing programs. Effects are really just small programs that take your clip and treat it with an effect, colour change or transition. This means you will have to wait to render the clip or wait for the computer to make the calculations, before you can see the result. However, with the right software and enough processing power – or a specialist video card designed to create and run video effects – you can watch this happen in realtime as you work. It's just that you may have to pay a lot for the privilege of not rendering yourself unconscious.

Apple's flagship software, Final Cut Pro, demonstrates what you should expect from a professional editing timeline. Multiple video tracks and a range of powerful features are important, but multiple audio tracks are just as essential.

Soft Options

Looking forwards to the edit, you may get frustrated by what the edit software has to offer with regard to plug-in applications. These are those little things in life that make your edit easier, or that simply nudge your Hollywood movie into a more professional realm.

STORYBOARDING SOFTWARE

These applications are not solely for those who can't draw. Today's storyboarding apps can imitate actors and camera moves, portray realistic lighting scenarios and create transitions between shots. If you really want to go the extra mile, they can even store and play dialogue and voice-over. In fact, your storyboard can become so much a whole movie in itself that you might not need to make your own Hollywood movie.

FX SOFTWARE

Effects apps are always tempting – a package of whizz-bang-zoom preset effects, often tailorable to suit your every moviemaking need. Whether they help your movie at all is another thing, and you also need to make sure they're compatible with your editing package.

Hollywood movies that get it right don't rely on effects to progress the story. While the antagonist might be a *Twister* or *Godzilla*, the story is always progressed by the actions and the dialogue, and the conflicts between antagonist and protagonist. An effects package probably won't contain a program to create effective, interactive freak weather conditions or towering monsters unless it's a specialist – and expensive – application. Instead, it'll contain a lot of effects that are fun to use, but which will probably be completely inappropriate to the progress of the story.

Real movie-effects packages are also pretty complex, so unless you have a lot of money to spend and time at your disposal, don't worry. There are far more useful things to have on your desktop.

CLEANERS AND ENCODERS

These items, for instance, are far more beneficial. A cleaner is a mixed bag of complicated algorithms that polish up your picture. If you want higher production values than your budget permits, then invest in a good cleaner/encoder.

They work by putting your digital data through the hoops and applying values which control the luminance and chrominance within preset ranges, resulting in a brighter, more colourful, balanced movie. Likewise, they treat audio to round off rough edges. They're not magic, but they're useful back-up tools to counteract any small errors of your own.

The encoder side of a cleaner allows all of this to take place, and transforms your movie into whatever format you require. Webstreaming, DVD, CD-ROM all require different types of compression. An encoder will transcode your AVI into another format if you need to – and a good encoder will do it using complicated sums that retain as much of the information in your images as it can.

SEQUENCERS AND MIXERS

Audio really is half the deal and getting it right shouldn't just be the job of edit software that would rather you look at the nice pictures. A sequencer can create all sorts of soundscapes that you couldn't even imagine. Better still, you don't have to be Mozart or The Neptunes to actually use it to your own ends.

Your edit software may well have a standard mixer as part of the application, and that will probably be good enough. Remember that if you are thinking about 5.1 stereo sound and the built-in mixer doesn't operate with it, it's the edit software you'll have to change to suit.

DVD AUTHORING SOFTWARE

It's likely that you'll want to burn your movie to DVD. Authoring software allows you to create menu

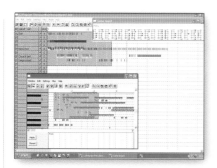

This kind of basic sequencer speaks, rings, bangs and warbles for itself – once you've put in a few notes of your own. The simplest sound you can come up with can become that one special element which gives a scene flavour and excitement.

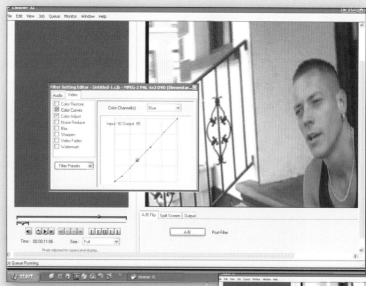

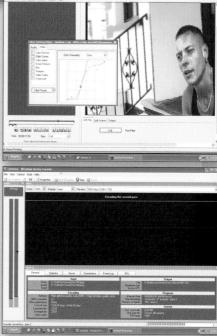

screens, chapter stops and – most importantly – it allows the disk to be played in domestic DVD players. Again, if you're using basic software, you won't get as much bang for your buck. If it's important that you have a polished product to sell, it's worth splashing out a bit more.

With ready-made themes and stylish templates, DVD authoring software can make all the difference to the presentation of your movie. Everyone admires an animated menu and it's a good way of introducing your work and getting an audience on your side from the start.

If you haven't got a colour corrector in your edit software, encoding software might be able to help. It's a good way to keep light and colour consistent across your movie, or grade entire scenes to create a mood. Stripping away colours, crushing blacks or changing hues can have a real impact.

preproduction

Introduction

Got all your gear? Time for the fun to begin. While most home moviemakers find preproduction a tiresome obstacle that gets in the way of picking up the camera and shooting, it's actually the one part of the entire process that'll make or break the movie.

Once you've got your space, the only thing you need is creativity. However, creativity needs ideas – and an empty space with no distractions never inspires the imagination. Stare at that blank screen for too long and it is only going to swallow you up. Instead, go and get your seed from the outside world and bring it into your space to germinate.

Preproduction is the backbone that holds everything together during shooting. How will you know if your movie shoot's a success? If it's on time and to budget, and you've got everything you want for the edit in the can. Getting that right takes some planning.

Your budget and the timeframe that you have to make your Hollywood movie are inextricable from one another. Time is money and money is time, for you, for your crew, for the actors, for all the third parties that you're going to come to rely on. There is never a time when money isn't being spent – and while it may not be coming directly out of your bank account, it certainly won't be going in.

Preproduction is all a matter of control. As long as things aren't out of your control, you're doing your job. But what is the job of a producer, and what makes a good one? If you look at Hollywood's producers, they need to be a lot of conflicting things simultaneously. Hard-nosed, but ingratiating; selfish, but giving; alienating, but friendly; terrier-like, but as warm and playful as a kitten. Good housekeeping and organization skills, attention to detail

and communication are the key to solid preproduction. You need to be able to take in the details, listen and understand. You will also need tact, diplomacy, wit, prudence, guile, eloquence, seduction and gut-feeling. If you are lacking in any of these departments, you'll need to get a handle on them pretty fast.

In order to bring out the best in yourself, find a space that's yours. It can be a home office, your edit

set-up, or any space that you can clear and call your own. In order to act professionally and come across as a viable investment, you've also got to be in a professional place mentally. If you're making calls asking for help and looking for sponsorship, it's always very difficult when somebody's hoovering around your feet – and you certainly won't be taken seriously on the other end of the line.

With everything at your fingertips, organized, with few distractions, you should be able to conduct yourself in a manner that wastes little time. The bare minimum that you should have in front of you at all times is a shoot and edit schedule, a list of contacts and a diary. There's a magic hour in everyone's day for 'doing stuff' and it tends to be between eight and nine in the morning. The magic hour is perfect for structuring your day so that you don't waste it. Franklin had it about right with his priority list, and there's absolutely nothing wrong with you allocating priorities (As, Bs, Cs) to the tasks in your diary if it ensures that the right stuff gets done in the day. Sometimes a tick can be the most satisfying thing in the world.

Focus is certainly the key to multi-tasking. As a producer, you're responsible for overseeing the whole of production, and that is difficult enough. As a producer/director/ writer, things can only get tougher. Suddenly, you're looking out from within, and it's very hard to make rational time and budget-saving decisions that way without being organized. Your job is going to get tough from time to time, but on a clear desk day, you can see forever.

A lot of ideas can come from your natural environment. Take your camera out for a walk and shoot a few people in a few locations. If you're stuck for inspiration, try and imagine what someone is doing in their location. What have they just done? What are they thinking or planning? What are they just about to do?

Hatching Your Plot

As you probably haven't got Tom Cruise or Julia Roberts on your payroll, the star of your Hollywood movie is going to have to be the story. It's the one thing that people will always come to see. And the thing that drives stories forwards is character.

Even the most complex movie story has a beginning, a middle and an end – though maybe not in that exact chronological order. The story also needs a resolution, and while that doesn't always mean a happy ending, it does need to end, and through a satisfying arc.

Hollywood story arcs come in threes, just like the classic novel, meaning there are three conflicts before the story is resolved. These conflicts are often obstacles in the way before a character can make a decision that triggers the climax and resolution. This is first base. Write down the income, the outcome and the three acts. By way of example:

- Income: Man invites guests to island to see homegrown dinosaurs
- Arc 1: Dinosaurs break loose and turn on the guests. Guests lost amidst the dinosaurs
- Arc 2: Guests find their way back to base to find it overrun by dinosaurs
- Arc 3: Guests outwit dinosaurs and escape with their lives
- Outcome: Guests go home

Each one of these three arcs creates an act – a traditional theatrical breakdown that is often confused in Hollywood convention with character arcs, the progress of characters as they change through each act. While the character arc remains a feature of the Hollywood machine (in the typical fish-out-of-water, coming-of-age plotlines etc), it's the story that affects the change.

Take your characters seriously, but they're not more important than the story. The characters are puppets; their purpose is to involve the audience in the narrative. For that time in front of your fake sets with your acting actors and your edited outtakes, you're trying to make an audience believe that what they are watching is real, and make them feel that the story is significant to the characters. Otherwise, why would you care? It sounds strange, but while your audience knows that what it's watching is fake, it also needs to feel that it's real.

There are ways to progress your story that don't involve characters at all. Once you've created your outline, instead of working with a character, work with your themes. Themes hold your movie together like glue, giving an audience a subconscious rope to hang onto as you pull them through your fake world. Themes, to Hollywood, can be as off-the-peg as proverbs, sayings and idioms (pride comes before a fall, absolute power corrupts absolutely, faint heart never won fair lady).

While generally regarded as clichés, these themes create quite traditional and easily comprehensible morality plays. Alternatively, themes can be a bit more global – 'identity', say, in *The Talented Mr. Ripley* or 'Christianity' in *RoboCop*. Because of the nature of the medium, though, themes can also be visual, such as the blur-out reflective moth-like transitions of *The Mothman Prophecies* or the increasing use of insipid yellow in *Rosemary's Baby*. These become visual clues used to strengthen the story.

Further, think about using aural themes. While any hero with any claim to being super will always have a musical theme, in *Jaws*, the shark's absence is hardly noticed because his da-dum theme represents his presence. Beyond music, while the jangling keys of Keys in *E.T.* are used to characterize him, thematically they also symbolize the prejudicial intent of man. And in *The Ring*, the telephone epitomizes the entire theme of the movie, semantically twisting the visual theme of the ring of light from within a closed well.

So, audio and musical themes are specifically used to identify characters and the nature of them, which brings us to your characters.

Once you've got your story, your arcs, your acts and your themes, work out whom you need to tell it to. Be harsh – characters cost time and money. Characters also need work to bring them to life. They need personality and motivation – and the best way of working them out is by putting yourself in their shoes. Remember, if their primary purpose is to drive the story, then their first *raison d'être* is always going to be to act. They either did or didn't do, or witnessed something. Whatever their involvement is, ask yourself these questions:

What would you do? How would you do it? Why would you do it? Who would you tell? Answering these questions will help you make the characters within your fake world believable. Believable characters have as many weaknesses as they do strengths – and flaws will create more dilemmas and more conflicts, and will propel the story more than any strength. Further, characters find strength through weakness or loss; just as, in reality, individuals learn from experience.

In the heightened reality of the Hollywood movie, it's the story elements consuming a character that drive their motivation and expose these strengths and weaknesses. Revenge, death, love, greed, lust, fear, hate – all of these things inspire a character and drive the story. Notice that it's only love which is generally perceived as a positive force. That's because it's conflict (standard good versus evil) that provides the core of the Hollywood story. Once the conflict is in place, it's a low probability of success, a character's inaction or a plot diversion that will takes the story through its three acts.

Reaction, in the fast-moving world of contemporary movies, is generally impulsive. That is to say that while Shakespeare would have characters pontificating, Hollywood tends to take this for granted and move a character on into action or reaction. Even with the grieving or lovelorn, audiences can be somewhat unforgiving and impatient and eventually end up despising the character that you're trying to gather empathy for.

Conflict allows your characters to react, and it's through reaction that the audience discovers the kind of personality your character has. Remember that if you're plotting well enough, your audience will be one step ahead in imagining what they would do in the same situation. While playing away from expectations can be more interesting, you – or your actor – has to give them a reason.

Stripping your plot of quiet moments, though, doesn't allow for pacing. Find moments that allow your audience to breathe by taking the edge off your characters, or by using your locations. Usually a good shot and some quiet, deliberate dialogue will let an audience catch up without sacrificing enjoyment.

Writing the Screenplay

Writing a script from your organized notes is equally formulaic, and there's a specific way of writing that makes acting, directing and shooting a whole lot easier for everyone. This format is available either through study or through software. Essentially it looks like this:

---

26. EXT. COLLEGE CAMPUS. DAY.

BLINKS bursts through both doors of the theatre's fire exit and strides ahead. DORA runs behind, trying to catch up with him. She loses pace, fumbling to find her sunglasses to temper the bright afternoon sun.

DORA
Hey, Blinks! Where are we going?

BLINKS (calling back)
Anywhere but here.

DORA
But what're we runnin' away from?

BLINKS (turning)
You're doing the running, Dor.

DORA catches up.

DORA
Hold up. You just walked outta that class.

BLINKS
And you followed me. It's your choice.

DORA
Don't gimme the shrug, Blinks.

BLINKS
I can't bear it in there. It's so...claustrophobic.

DORA
Blinks, you can't just walk outta class.

BLINKS
So what do you think we are doing? Stay cool, Dor. The others'll be out soon anyway.

DORA glances over her shoulder. BARBIE, TAKES, and TAROT are strolling in their direction. BARBIE grins and puts her Chanel shades on. TAKES and TAROT simply look exasperated.

DORA
Hey Barbie! Takes! Tarot!

BLINKS blinks again.

DORA
You knew.

BLINKS (shrugging)
People just do what they want to do. Oh, and I know where we're going now.

DORA
Where?

BLINKS
Right here.

Their stroll has brought them to a children's playground. Blinks climbs up a ladder and slides down the slide.

TAROT (from a distance)
Cool, man. We skippin' to play funnies?

TAROT comes running over with BARBIE. They're both squealing childishly, hand in hand. TAKES walks sombrely behind. TAROT pulls BARBIE onto the roundabout and spins them both around, laughing.

BLINKS (to DORA)
You see? Now how much more creative are we being?

DORA grins back.

DORA
Look at Takes.

They BOTH squint into the sun. TAKES is getting onto the swing. He pushes himself off from the ground with his feet, then swings higher and higher.

BLINKS
Hey, Takes! You having fun?

TAKES doesn't reply. He keeps swinging and swinging...

If you've based your story on arcs, acts, themes and characters, you should have no problem writing a script, because you've already done all the hard work. The antithesis of this easiness is trying to synopsize a prewritten source, which takes a lot of incisive paring and comprehension to put together. Actually, if you are interpreting somebody else's work, then remember that that is exactly what it is: an interpretation. You don't think the way they think or write the way they write, so don't even try. Come up with your own version; take the plot, characters and themes that first made an impression on you and evolve them into something personal enough to keep your interest.

Whichever way you're writing, the key is always in the first five pages. An A4 page, double-spaced, will work out at about a minute's screen-time, and the first five minutes of any movie on screen is critical to grab attention. To do this, your opener has to raise questions that are too intriguing to be ignored. From classic 'whodunit?' to 'whoisit?', 'whydidtheydothat?,' 'whatsgoingon?' 'wherearethey?' to current FX-led 'howdidtheydothat?', the key is to provide an intro strong enough and intriguing enough to keep an audience in their seats. This, of course, is becoming more and more of a precredits sequence, which often gives the first five minutes over to pure thrills.

When you're writing your opener, it doesn't have to introduce your lead character. It doesn't even have to have anything to do with your plot until the story ties up. This is a tried-and-tested device to keep an audience watching, relying on the psychology that an ending doesn't have to be happy, it doesn't have to be hugely climactic, it just has to be satisfying. If all the significant characters are in the right physical space and mental place, having lived and learned with the audience and saying all the right and apt things, then you've got yourself a satisfying ending. Oh, and conventional 'good' and 'bad' don't necessarily count in a good screenplay.

When describing characters, don't paint yourself into a corner with specifics. Keep it general enough to make casting as wide an open call as you can. While 'puberty hit hard and fast' (*Eight-Legged Freaks*) requires only a sex, age and temperament ('nerd'), the story might require the addition of an essential physical element ('a well-crafted swastika on his chest' – *American History X*).

Throughout the course of the script, don't feel as though you have to overexplain, especially with dialogue. Think of your script as a comic book where you are writing the words to pictures that do most of the work. If you're the director writing, you'll probably know how much is explained with dialogue and how much is explained in visuals. If this isn't the case, be kind and provide enough information in short descriptive passages.

A lot of good scriptwriting allows the audience to be party to certain clues along the way. Knowing things that the characters don't know treads a fine line between audience frustration at a character's stupidity or obliviousness and creating thrills and spills. Allowing an audience access to information can be done suggestively or overtly. You can be suggestive by creating a mood with lighting, shots and audio; overt by playing out a scene which shows that something is around the corner. This sense of the predictive is an extremely important tool to the scriptwriter. Remember how stupid you felt rewatching *The Sixth Sense*? The dialogue wasn't even a clue: it was a dead giveaway.

Another way of keeping writing easy is to structure your scenes as you would imagine them cut. Long scenes don't exist much any more, mostly because impatient audiences don't like them. Structured within a pacy piece, though, rhythm can be created. Keeping every scene short with humdinger lines and killer looks at the end just turns your movie into an abridged soap opera. It's the combination of pace, breathing space and beats between lines that create the rhythm of a script.

After writing your script, you can introduce your symbolism – visual extensions of your themes. If your theme is resurrection, think about a lens flare that briefly creates halos or window gobos that throw forehead crosses on your character. Think also about the way that each scene plays against the next and the previous. What links them? Is there a way of making a transition from one to another easier on the eye or the brain? Is it something someone says that is answered in the next line? Or is it something that becomes an irony by the next scene?

Now it's time to shake things up. If you have created a world that makes sense, then you can take a new angle and deconstruct it. That means thinking about Hollywood convention and rerooting your story in its own time and space. Is there a scene that would work better in a different place? Are you working forwards in time when your movie would be more interesting played backwards? Does it need to move forward chronologically to progress?

It's also time to think about audio themes – and again, that doesn't just mean music, but feel. Mention sounds or audio in the script if you feel as though it adds a potent mood or, again, irony to the scene.

TREATMENT

Writing scripts is a complicated-enough process, even if you know where you're going. For this reason, synopses and treatments exist. A synopsis is a customary method of putting an idea across in order to sell the concept of your movie. In broadcast television, this is done before a script is commissioned - and in movies, generally after the script is written. Either way, it requires skill to ensure that it's concise enough while containing the right balance of detail and clarity to make it appealing for sponsorship or distribution.

Genre and Drama

Genres are incredibly important to an audience. Within the art world there are media (literary, theatrical, painting etc.), methods (cut-up, watercolour) and genres (epic, tragic, romantic). Because an audience is made up of a global demographic, genres allow for art to be tailored to specific groups within that demographic. In the cinema, genre is dependent on the story.

With moviemaking – like any other medium – different genres attract different audiences. A lot of directors tend to work within their own areas (Hitchcock: Suspense; Capra: Whimsical Fantasy; John Ford: Western; De Mille: Epic). This leads to entire genres being Hitchcockian, Capra-esque and so on. What each of them has in common, however, is that they are all telling a story.

Some directors work completely across genre. Ang Lee has managed to work successfully with period drama, western and comic book; Spielberg with horror, war, sci-fi, period drama and caper. More than this, genre hybrids have emerged. *Star Wars* was described as a 'western in space', *Titanic* is a love story in a disaster movie wrapped as an epic. Most genres incorporate at least one other subgenre. War movies can be set in space, fantasies can be musicals, action movies can be shot as film noir. Let this make your movie different.

To give you more options, every story is told with a method. This is not the genre, but the language in which it is told – the techniques used to tell that kind of story. It is not the use of dark shadows and blinding whites, obscure low angles and porkpie hats that make a movie noir, but themes of moral darkness, crime and sexual obsession. These methods – these recognizable languages – can be taken over to other genres. For instance, noir conventions were transposed to sci-fi with *Blade Runner*, so fashioning a specific conceit.

Note that drama doesn't quite make the grade to genre. Every Hollywood movie is, by nature, dramatic. Every story has a drama – a conflict, no matter how big or small. Any reference to drama as a genre is really about having a miscellaneous can to dump question mark movies into: the *Ordinary People*/movie of the week bracket.

Drama

Conflict is drama, and drama is everything to the Hollywood movie. So how do you go about creating it? Conflict in a Hollywood movie can be verbal, physical, personal, visual or editorial. If it's verbal, it's the script that's responsible. Whether it's a disagreement or an argument, there are various ways of heightening or dulling the effect. Increasing or decreasing that tension is entirely dependent on the global or story arc. If the conflict is about to develop into a fight sequence, it has to be a pretty dramatic conflict, but if the conflict is about to end with someone walking out of a room, it has to be contained.

To contain verbal conflict is a question of direction. Instead of delivery with all guns blazing, try getting your actors down to a whisper. This is a good way of actually making the lines more venomous, more deliberate. Hearing characters railing loudly soon becomes annoying for an audience – it doesn't allow your characters to have shades of grey. Temper your tempers if you want to succeed.

The same goes with the physical representation. If a fight is building, the visual signs of a conflict should escalate slowly or suddenly, grow or burst into the action. In drama, you may well not have actual fighting. It might be that you just want to express a character's aggressiveness or defensiveness – the two extremes of conflict.

Think of your characters' surroundings. What would they fiddle with? Pick up? Crumple? Throw? Seating a character contains them in the scene: if they stand from seating, make it an important line or a challenge. If they're free-roaming, it implies a lack of containment and self-restraint. The character becomes more threatening and unpredictable.

And here's the deal: threat and unpredictability don't have to pay off with action. If you establish what your character is capable of in conflict once, their potential menace stays with the audience. Think of *Blue Velvet*'s Frank or *American Beauty*'s Lester Burnham as extreme characters who use restraint and only occasionally explode. With a volatile personality, the steady build-up of tension can be so exciting or terrifying that you don't always need the violent release.

Personal conflict is something that most protagonists have in spades. You can do it with words, whether voice-over (Tracy Flick in *Election*), verbal schizophrenia (Gollum/Smeagol in *The Two Towers*) or simply in conversation. You can also represent it visually. Props can be a nifty way of constructing drama from your characters. *The Shining*'s Jack Torrance types the same phrase incessantly, while *Fatal Attraction*'s Alex Forrest repeatedly flicks the light switch to portray variant levels of madness. Staring into a cracked mirror or smearing make-up might suit your character better.

If you've got plot, characters and a location, you can turn that into drama. Use the surroundings to set the mood, write the dialogue to match it, then put your actors through their paces. Build conflict and tension, and you keep your audience interested.

Genre 1	Genre 2	Method	Movie
War	Bio-Pic	Realist	*Schindler's List*
Spy	Family	Live-action cartoon	*Spy Kids*
Sci-Fi	Comedy	Musical	*The Rocky Horror Picture Show*
Fantasy	Rom-Com	Animation	*Shrek*
Thriller	Crime	Noir	*Se7en*
Mystery	Thriller	Surrealist	*Mulholland Drive*
Period	Bio-Pic	Expressionist	*Shadow of the Vampire*
Road	Chick Flick	Romanticist	*Thelma and Louise*
Musical	Weepie	Dogme	*Dancer in the Dark*
Western	Horror	Comedy	*From Dusk Till Dawn*
Arthouse	Adult	Hyper-realist	*Baise-Moi*
Martial Arts	Sci-Fi	Fetishist	*The Matrix*

Moving the Plot Along

Beyond genre conventions and classic storytelling, Hollywood has many ways of moving the plot through the film. Whether you want to reuse them or rework them, you can use these in your own screenplay.

Time in this scene is represented by The Waiting Game. The subject is waiting for the phone to ring, meaning that she has to sweat it out as an obstacle – the police – gets nearer.

ACTION

Action is incredibly easy for the scriptwriter. It's one of those things that sits in a page without taking up much space: 'THEY fight', 'SHE chases him around the house with a chainsaw', or 'HE uses the SPOON to unlock his handcuffs and dig his way out of the cell'.

It's not that easy for the director, though, and any action sequence is worth storyboarding first. Like dialogue, action sequences are all about giving an audience all of the parts they need to understand – to make sense of – the scene.

Subjects, objectives and obstacles

Your subject is your protagonist, antagonist or whichever character is the centre of the action. To create a believable action sequence, your actor's responsibility is to act and react as if their situation were real. It's half the battle to give your action personality.

The way to do this is to get your audience involved and let your subject act and emote true to the given circumstance. Even with an antagonist, the audience will expect them to act as if they mean to win or survive (aggressive) or escape (defensive). These are natural human traits, and it's very seldom that a character will be apathetic or suicidal in action unless given suitable motivation.

The subject in the action doesn't have to be heroic. Think of Indiana Jones' wry resignation to shooting the swordsman, or Bruce Willis' 'wrong guy in the wrong place at the wrong time' in the *Die Hard* movies. What you're shooting, then, is not just the action, but the motivation and subsequent emotion behind the actions.

The objective is what your subject has to do that provides the action, whether it's getting away from the bad guys or escaping a burning house. This objective has to be made clear from the start. And while objectives can be alluded to in dialogue, the conclusion needs to be described visually. Remember Annie Wilkes' big bugbear about cliffhangers in *Misery?* An audience hates a nontelegraphed conclusion.

Obstacles lie between the subject and the accomplishment of the objective, providing the conflict and creating the action. These are cars, pedestrians, bridges or buildings in car chases, or the locked doors and flaming staircases that stop your subject from getting out of a flaming house. Once you've got subject, objective and obstacle, you've got conflict and reaction, which equals action. Just remember: your audience hates cheating, and loathes an unsatisfying conclusion. If, after a huge action conflict, the obstacle is beaten by default or the subject accomplishes their objective by accident, you will be booed out of the cinema.

SUSPENSE

Suspense can be a race or chase, a will-they-won't-they, a whodunit or a mystery unravelled – what matters is that it keeps the audience 'hanging' with a question: will your protagonist reach their goal in time, discover who did do it in time or unravel what happened in time?

Time is the real antagonist in suspense, and manifests as many things. Sometimes it's absolutely literal: a ticking clock or timebomb. While this might have hit absolute cliché, there are always ways to subvert it. *Nick of Time* plays the suspense out as real time (one minute for one minute), *D.O.A.* gives the protagonist poison and forty-eight hours to work out what happened to him before he dies, and *Memento* plays each scene in reverse order.

A ticking clock can be something else entirely: a car that won't start with the killer close behind, or an open safe with a security guard passing by. Suspense requires the protagonist to act in time before it's too late, or to avoid awful consequences for a period of time.

In the average Hollywood movie, we know, deep down, that the protagonist will succeed. This is exactly why creating conflicts is so important. They can be dramatic red herrings to distract an audience from a predictable outcome, or the one element that drives the entire plot can be a type of red herring – the Hitchcock-coined McGuffin. A plot-enabling device that is inconsequential to the actual story, a McGuffin tends to be either a prop

(the glowing briefcase in *Pulp Fiction*) or information (the NOC list in *Mission Impossible*). The McGuffin becomes the thing that everyone wants (race), that somebody has (chase) or that nobody appears to have (mystery). Putting in an object to act as your McGuffin is a quick way to make your story arc work. 'What's in the suitcase?' is a tried and tested way of causing conflict between protagonists and antagonists.

The mysterious suitcase with the secret contents is the classic McGuffin. The audience doesn't really need to know what's inside it. All it needs to know is that everybody in the film wants it.

SHOCKS AND SCARES

Horror takes conflict to an extreme, stacking the odds against the protagonist. Horror doesn't always have to involve the culling of your cast on video, and the balance is always giving the audience what they want (scares, death, a story) while surprising them.

Working successfully, horror does more than just scare us – it confronts us with base-level fears. Horror both employs and undermines conventions in order to unsettle or shock the audience. If it's the typical serial-killer chiller, you just need a cast and a lot of blood to make the movie, but you need sympathetic characters and a memorable antagonist to make that movie work. Putting that combination in ordinary circumstances that

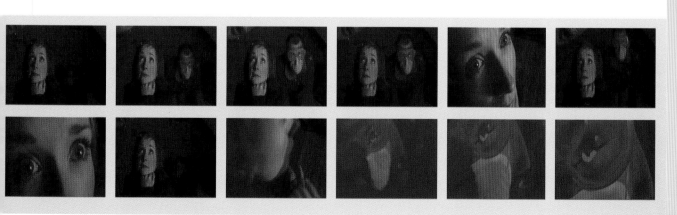

suddenly turn horrific will make it feel real. Even a gory body horror movie won't be shocking with cardboard characters in a cardboard world.

Stories of the supernatural and the occult work on a more subtle level, but that makes problems of its own. Making ghosts believable can be tough, and how does a transparent or unseen ghost have any physicality to do anything? If it doesn't kill, then how many times can you say 'boo' before your audience realizes that that's the limit of its powers?

For these reasons, the occult works best within another storyline altogether. *The Others* is about the spiralling madness of a mother; *The Exorcist* is about a fatherless pubescent; *Rosemary's Baby* is about the fear of pregnancy; *Poltergeist* is about the loss of a child... Notice a theme here? Each one is still just a horror movie.

LAUGHS

Comedy is a funny business. It's almost impossible to get it right for everyone. Like a horror movie – scary to some, not to others – it may or may not work according to the individual's experience and personality. What some find hilarious, others will dismiss as trite. And the bad news? Your audience is made up of many individuals.

Luckily, while Hollywood comedy has to appeal to the masses, with an easily digestible, broadspread type of humour, your comedy can be more fine-tuned. If you find something funny and think an audience might agree, tell it that way.

Our hero carries on blithely as violence erupts in the foreground. Slapstick, taste-free, offbeat or black comedy? It's all in the writing, the performances and the style. Funny? That's up to your audience to decide.

The good thing about comedy is that it can form a hybrid with just about any other genre, the romantic comedy being the most usual. There are also some distinct types of comedy, from slapstick to black comedy. Here's a breakdown:

Slapstick
Ludicrous situation comedy (script-led), coupled with overt visual gags such as cream pies and banana skins, and conducted with an extraordinary amount of incompetence, clumsiness and bungling. Slapstick needs good actors who are fundamentally performance artists. If you don't have any rubber faces with rubber limbs in your troupe, you might just find someone who makes you laugh in your crew.

Taste-free
Body fluids, sex and sexuality, religion and anything non-politically correct shown with no restraint. Taste-free uses visual gags around

unwitting characters. *There's Something About Mary* taught Hollywood a lesson here: if you're going to do it, do it with a proper story and proper characters.

Think about taking a normal romantic-comedy script and working a bit of taste-free into it. There are plenty of sticky sides to dating, so let your imagination run riot. Throw yourself into it, too – no audience is going to thank you for being coy.

Gentle comedy
Romantic comedy, situation comedy, learning-to-love-yourself and general joie-de-vivre form the large part of white-bread generic Hollywood dramas with lightweight scripts. There aren't often many visual gags in gentle comedy, which relies more on a script that is simple and simplistic in its view of life – if not unrealistic. The comedy, here, will be in the writing and will rely on your main and supporting talent to be likeable and adept in their execution. Think Meg Ryan-fluffy, Tom Hanks-affability or Reese Witherspoon-ditzy.

Offbeat comedy
Offbeat deals with subjects that aren't instantly amusing with characters who aren't necessarily funny. While it tends to defy specific

genre or hybrid, it also tends to deal with the dysfunctional. All audiences now understand dysfunction to be the Real World – the world that they themselves come from – and offbeat serves as the flipside to gentle comedy: the level of comedy is the same, but there's a darkness to the portrayal of the world.

If you've got these characters and situations in your script, try and look at it in a different way: maybe the world on the page isn't odd but is funny because it's real.

Black comedy

Black comedy goes one step further, and situation comedy created from the most unpleasant story can work beautifully. Murder, death, bizarre sexual antics – anything that you'd rather not talk about in front of grandma is perfect.

Again, this is in the writing. The fact is not that audiences won't go and see anything dark without a trace of humour – they will. The fact is that laughing at the horrific and the tragic is a cathartic and guilty pleasure in a poker-faced, strait-laced world. This is taste-free humour without the comfort of gags. What's so funny? Is it too vulgar or brutal to be funny? Only you and your actors can decide.

ROMANCE

Boy meets girl, boy loses girl, boy gets girl. Love the cliché or hate it, it happens the world over, and it happens most in Hollywood.

Audiences love to believe in the idea that we are all destined to love and be loved. This doesn't mean that romance needs a happy ending. An unhappy romantic Hollywood movie ending is not regarded as unsatisfying if the story requires it: it's bittersweet or it's realistic – and it's certainly permissible.

Just as unhappiness is allowed, so is unfair play. Romance usually requires that one or more temporary partners be rejected, and the audience is excused from liking these perimeter characters because they're portrayed to be flawed or unsuitable, or just a little bit boring. The stars are aligned for the happy couple and woe betide any character that stops them getting together.

Nothing in the real world, though, is straightforward, and even Hollywood romance needs conflict – something that keeps the couple separated, if only for a while. Maybe her dad doesn't approve, he's getting married or there are age or class differences. The course of true love never runs smooth.

Also, your characters need to be believable, and that goes whether they're shy, gregarious, vulnerable or wild, and whether you put them at college, in a courtroom, in beatnik New York or in a mental institute.

Your couple also need interesting quirks and a sense of balance. If she's bold and he's shy, give her a flaw (physical clumsiness) and him a strength (he can add up the price of cocktails before the waitress) to temper them. It can even be best if those traits work against each other. When couples are both happy on screen at the same time, the audience reaches for the bucket. This is why couples spend most time apart on screen (conflict = drama) and when they are getting along, it works better if they're sparring – and that is the job of a good script.

Yet again, conflict creates sparks – in this case romance. Try this from *Ocean's Eleven*:

- Does he make you laugh?
- He doesn't make me cry.
Or
- I'm not joking.
- I'm not laughing.

Conflict means there has to be emotion – and with the right delivery, you know it must be love.

Drawing on Ideas

Storyboards are your next stop to finalizing the way that you want to shoot your Hollywood movie. While the actors have their scripts and the producer has the shooting schedule, the most important reference material that you'll need is your storyboard.

During the pandemonium of the shoot, it'll be your best friend and greatest ally, reassuring you that you've got all the shots you're going to need to make sense of the story. With pictures, words and strategies, it's the closest you'll get to experiencing the actual movie.

Your storyboard is a visualization of what you see when reading the script. If you wrote the script, you're ahead of the game and probably had locations, shots and angles in mind when you wrote it. If you didn't, now is the time to make the movie your own – or at least tell it from your own perspective.

Making sure that you are telling the story is the most important thing about a storyboard, and you need to do so without any wild ideas that will blow both your time and your budget. Because the storyboard is a cross-off list for your shots and a visual reference to the script while shooting, there's no point in putting in crane shots and exploding cars if you don't have the budget to do it. Think simply: what shots do you need, at minimum, to describe what is happening within each scene.

The most important thing from the start is that you don't have to be an artist – in fact, you don't actually have to be able to draw. Stick-people bearing no resemblance to human beings in landscapes with a perspective not seen since *Alice In Wonderland* are absolutely fine. Always remember that while a storyboard is a good show-and-tell for the camera op and actors, it's fundamentally there for you. And you understand it, because you drew it. The things that you do have to be are:

Respectful of the story

Don't start chucking in erratic symbolism or revealing flashbacks to make your mark on the script when they're either going to detract from the story or ruin the ending. Know where the story is going, what each scene is there for, and tell it like it is.

Well-versed in the language of shots

Know when to use your close-up, your reaction shot, your establisher and so on. Make sure that they're in the right order to reveal or conceal the intention, motivation and progression of the scene. If it's a dialogue scene that you're storyboarding, keep the 180° rule in mind – as well as working around lighting rigs, audio and crew.

Familiar with your locations

A wide may be impossible on your quarry lunar landscape when there's an obvious industrial estate in the background. Similarly, while a wrong-doing character staring out of the window onto a portentious church might read well, your producer might not have been so lucky in finding such a vista.

So, it's all down to time and money and being informed.

While the compositions of your storyboard are important, you're not creating a comic. This is going to be a motion picture and the movements of actors and vehicles within scenes, as well as the camera itself, need to be described on paper if you want to know in advance how each separate shot will work, and how they will work with or against each other in the edit. Use arrows to indicate movement to connect your series of static images. At least let an inanimate storyboard have the chance of being dynamic.

The audio is just as integral as the visuals of each shot. Make a note of dialogue or any particular sound effect under each image to complete the explanation of the shot.

If any further explanation is needed to support your words and pictures, write it in. Indicate use of lighting, or where you anticipate a mic might be hidden. These notes are part of your strategy to save time on the set. Your storyboard is your ammunition in the time/budget battlezone of production. Check shots off as you shoot and you'll benefit from a sense of achievement.

DARK MARKET : PRE-TITLE SEQUENCE.

SLOW FADE FROM BLACK
S/O : HEAVY BREATHLESS
BREATHING

FRANTIC HAND-HELD TRACK
OF CU FEET RACING OVER FLOOR
STUDIO V/O : FIRST TWO LINES "... OUTSIDE ..."

CUT TO:

LS LOCK OFF : SILHOUETTE
PASSES THROUGH FRAME
(DAY FOR NIGHT?)
STUDIO V/O : 2ND TWO LINES "... CAN'T SEE ..."

CU HAND-HELD OF DOLL, EYES
OPENING/CLOSING WITH MOTION
STUDIO V/O : "... WHO WANTS TO RUN
FOR FEAR OF ME ..."

CUT TO:

HAND-HELD PUSH-IN THEN PAN
TO REVEAL CLIFF EDGE
STUDIO V/O : LAST 2 LINES "... WITH ME ..."

HAND-HELD TOPSHOT : CLIFF EDGE
STUDIO V/O : "INSIDE ..."

CUT TO:

PUSH IN TO

REVERSE!

Location, Location, Location

If you're shooting guerrilla-fashion, you can skip this section. Guerrilla filmmaking is like going on holiday. Holidays are not there 'to get away from it all': they're there to enable you to treat somebody else's property with complete disregard to pursue your own entertainment. These pages are about treating a foreign environment well and getting what you want from it.

Don't get it wrong. Your locations are vital for four fundamental reasons. First and foremost, they will take up a critical part of your time and budget. Rigging, prepping, rehearsing talent and crew, shooting and derigging take time—much more time than a shot is really worth in your movie. Once you add in the transport of gear, crew and talent to the spot, not to mention any troubleshooting required, running off for batteries, getting tape, snacks and transport back, going on location can take a huge amount of time and energy from your available resources.

However, all that hassle might be worth it. A location can define the personality of the movie. The desert in *Thelma and Louise* becomes a barren, eternal theme for their lives and deaths; in *The Evil Dead*, the woods are quite literally alive with the sound of screaming.

Cheap shoots

When you find a location, the best-case scenario is that it offers everything for nothing.

This kind of scenario is difficult – but not impossible – to find. Usually, you'll need to rely on someone to fix your location for you. This might be someone who owns a flat or a press officer for the site or the caretaker of a school. These are the people that you need to have on side to get the shots that you want. Meet with them, talk them through your intentions on set and how it will be used in the story, promise them a credit. Really, flattery and celebrity by proxy can get you things that you want for absolutely nothing. But while credits are free, some locations are not.

If your contact or company has wised-up – that is, the location has been used and abused by film crews in the past – then they might charge a location fee. This can be anything from a small charity donation to an expensive daily fee. Obviously, this puts pressure on your budget and your time, which means you need to make a judgment call on whether it is worth your time and money to proceed. If money is an issue, look at your script. Does it really need that location? Is there another one that would do?

Trading places

Like characters, locations can be changed – and the movie can get itself a new personality. If you are planning on swapping locations when faced with fees, let your contact know. Making a decision not to shoot there can be leverage for getting what you want – if they don't want publicity in a movie that might go big on the amateur scene, then there is bound to be someone else who will. Sometimes location fees are tried out on professional producers in order to play the prima

---

LOCATION LOGISTICS

When you find a location, the best-case scenario is that it offers everything for nothing. *Everything* consists of the following:

- A variety of usable angles and open shooting parameters
- Electricity for cameras, batteries, lights
- Shops for food, water, tapes, lights, beer, fuel
- Accommodation if anyone needs to stay over
- Freedom to shoot what you want in peace

Nothing is:

- No payment

donna game. If Joel Silver wouldn't take it, why should you?

If the criterion for using a location is publicity for the company, then listen to what they want and find a compromise. It's not in your interests to have logos behind your actors, but you're not Ridley Scott, there needs to be something in it for the owners. Find a compromise and steer them towards a credit. If they find the whole thing too 'impossible' – or too much like hard work – reassure them that the time that you require is minimal. Don't lie, or you'll end up with a number of useless shots and a bad reputation to boot.

Instead, find some compromise in your script that requires a shorter shoot; storyboard and rehearse tightly enough to just require a first take and a safety; ensure your actors arrive in full make-up and costume; get your camera op to shoot your wide shots and cutaways while you prepare your actors, and get ready to shout, 'action!'

Once you're there – with approval and an understanding – the most important thing is to keep your cast and crew happy. If you can get a runner or two for the day, then this is the day to do it on. While shooting on location is exhilarating, it can also be demanding, and your runners can get to the shops and back for food, batteries, tapes and props while you get another shot.

One final word of advice: always build in time to leave a location the way that you found it. If you need to go back for reshoots, the last thing you need is a bad reputation and a closed door.

If you can't afford to stage your own pagan ritual, borrow somebody else's. Taking actors along to a firework display and performing with enough distance from the general public for audio and defocused images saves both time and money.

Shooting on beaches can be interesting. Check for tides to make sure you're not going to leave your lead stranded. A lot of beaches are private, some are naturist, and all of them have every element against you shooting anything. With sand in your servo, sea in your lens and wind blowing your talent's dress around, least you're likely to be near a corner shop.

Exterior locations are everywhere. Every major town has a few public spaces or official buildings that can lend gravitas to your movie, as long as you can find a quiet moment.

Setting Scenes

While locations give your movie a sense of natural scope and believability, using sets is a more controlled and artificial approach. This doesn't mean using a set has to be at the expense of credibility, though. And neither does it have to look cheap and tatty. In fact, a well-dressed and lit set can really raise your production values.

A set is any shooting space that has to be artificially lit and dressed in order to become your actors' new world. Locations are often out of the filmmaker's control due to nature (weather, daylight, night hours) or practical aspects (time, budget, batteries). Sets, on the other hand, have no weather conditions or limited daylight hours, they have electricity, and are free from all natural phenomena (and that includes members of the public lurking in the back of your shot).

Sets are usually interiors, but can be studios dressed as exteriors. This is happening more often in Hollywood's higher budget bracket in order to have the same amount of control 'outdoors' as indoors. The richness that exterior daytime locations add to a movie is a result of one of nature's gifts to film-makers: natural light. Recreating natural light or working with artificial light on set is another thing altogether, and make or break as far as your light-sensitive images look.

Your budget probably isn't going to allow for exteriors to be shot in a studio. Your sets, therefore, are more likely to be interior rooms that need to be lit and dressed to recreate the interior rooms in the story of your movie. Fine. There are plenty of rooms in the world that'll do this, and they may even be in your own house. The hardest part is to take your room, pull it out of the cheap everyday and make it into a spectacular environment that is practical to work in.

In order to create depth and make the room work as a set, it's got to be reasonably proportioned. When shooting a movie, it's usual that you'll want to establish the room dimensions at some point. The smaller the room, of course, the less successful this is going to be. Consider the use of lights and the whereabouts of cameras, cables and crew, and suddenly your options for actually moving your people and props about diminish. The feeling of claustrophobia is better faked.

A room is just that until you fill it, then it starts to become a set. Props make what is conventional become credible, and dressing a set can be the most fun part of your shoot. If your budget doesn't allow for art directors, set-dressers and buyers, then at least the fun is all yours.

Reference the time and place to create the believable. Historical sets are always the most difficult to get right, for while there is attainable history all around (houses, antiques markets), there are plenty of people in your audience who probably know eras better than you do. Decide whether it's cheaper (in budget and time) to 'borrow' an eighteenth-century house or fill a nineteenth-century house with antiques. Dressing, though, doesn't just mean tables and chairs. All the obvious things – walls, ceilings, and floors – are sometimes just too in-your-face to notice...until you get to the edit.

Present-day (or near to) is a little easier on your time – and car boot sales are cheaper. The future, fantastically, hasn't been written. This is great news for your creativity and, potentially, your budget. Avoid the *Logan's Run* trap, though. You don't want to 'put the future back thirty years' – as reviewers said at the time – and even sci-fi spoofs (*Galaxy Quest* or *Spaceballs*) hardly paint egg cartons silver...

If the combination of sets, props and dressing looks too hard on your budget, change your script. *Romeo + Juliet* had no problems working in contemporary LA from a prewritten source, and there's no reason why your movie should either. If you've got a tight set and don't need much in the way of materials, send off for samples or swatches of fabric, tiles, paint – whatever it takes. It's free.

The other version of 'free' is to find a store that's got what you want to borrow and offer them a credit

Five minutes' worth of make-up, wardrobe and set-dressing can make all the difference if you're using your own room. Natural daylight can be very cold and very unforgiving for digital video and even a practical standard lamp just adds that extra bit of warmth to the shot.

Hiring more elaborate sets may just need a bit more charm. If you're looking for a bar or restaurant, try and find one that has a private function room. While anything that can be bought by the hour is a bonus, go and see it at the time that you're going to shoot and make sure that you're going to get the audio that you want and not just some 'wisdom' from the raucous drunks upstairs.

There are sets out there waiting to be used. Theatres - especially the small, local variety - often have sets hanging around to be derigged. And they have lights. Using something preconstructed for the afternoon is generally cheap, if not free. Your only consideration will be the theatre's likely safety policy, so try and find a day where there's at least a stage-hand or technician around.

for the favour. Sometimes being cheeky will get you everywhere. Shops close down too. and while that's bad news for them, it can be good news for you. Don't forget rubbish tips and salvage yards, either. These will often have the stuff of history for less money than a proper antiques dealer, and – with a friendly request or some financial incentive – any unwanted items left for disposal can be put aside for you.

Some sets just need light to bring them back to life. If you can get your hands on maintenance tunnels for a public institution, it doesn't take much to turn them into an atmospheric location.

Use whatever you can get hold of to make your set work in your movie. Take the lighting that's there, and add to it. if you can find a disused building to shoot in, you can add decor and materials to bring it to life.

PREPRODUCTION

Stars and Actors

A true star inspires everyone around them. They create energy and life on set and make other people feel good. There are plenty of people who do this without being actors. If you're a good director, you'll do this too.

Your actors are divided into leads, supporting, walk-ons and extras – not stars and everybody else. A happy cast is made up of people all being treated in the same way and it's a director's skill that can do this. Of course, if you do happen to enlist a familiar face – much to your own amazement – you might feel obliged to fall over yourself with obsequiousness. Try not to. Your name talent may not even want or require this attention, and your energies should not be spent at the expense of your other actors.

Actors are a strange breed. They know this – they feel different because they're paid to be somebody else – and they play upon it as celebrity, whatever their status. Being a director is knowing when to undermine this, and when to go with it. It's people-person time. The point is to always look for that actor in the character and not for the character in the actor. And the reason for this is that whatever depth you've prescribed for your character, your actor is a real-life person...and can bring more than you've ever imagined.

Your script will have defined roles. Maybe your character is 21, blonde, with a knockout figure, but be kind to yourself. Look at your viable options when it comes to casting. If you've only got brunettes, don't dye their hair – look at the character in a different light instead. The same goes with age, and even sex. The measure for this is that *Alien*'s Ripley was initially envisaged as a male ('Roby', sex-changed to make the character more interesting), and the rest of the cast didn't have any predefined gender whatsoever.

Your script may be written with friends in mind who've already agreed to play their parts. In this case, you're lucky. If you think that you're professional enough to put out a request for headshots before auditioning, that's pretty lucky too. Usually, though, the answer is by holding open casting calls.

If you're putting out an open casting call, describe the character and not the kind of actor that you're looking for. Actors know when they are not right for roles. Believe them. If they don't believe it themselves, your chances of creating something believable is next to nothing. Unlike the description in the script, yours should be generic, and unless you need an action hero or a burly giant, try not to be physically specific. The bookish duckling that transforms into the prom queen is always the swannish actor underneath.

Don't be afraid to hold auditions. There are plenty of wannabe actors and resting actors out there who really don't mind giving their time for something worthwhile...for nothing. Actors who want something else on their cv will just ask for a showreel videotape from your production. These actors, though, tend to be within a certain age group – i.e. early twenties – which can either limit the scope of your production, or lead to, sometimes healthy, further drafts of the script.

The Internet is a marvellous means of finding talent. There are a lot of sites out there that exist to promote small-budget productions. If you've got the talent, try creating your own site with preproduction marketing graphics, taglines and teasers. This is very useful if you want to attract online interest and convey your seriousness about your production. There are plenty of fair-weather directors out there, so convincing actors that your Hollywood movie is worth their while will at least open up the number of applicants.

Arrange to see the same character applicants on the same day to keep things relative and in perspective. It's much easier to make decisions this way, if you're fortunate enough to have enough applicants to make any decisions necessary.

If you are thinking about some kind of public disibution, each actor – even extras – should be given a contract or release form. While there are standard pro-forma contracts around, the choice of wording is up to you, and it's all to do with

Most working actors – unless they're stars – will have a cv. This is a generally a terribly out-of-date picture, a biography and their physical statistics. If they can do accents and juggle at the same time, this will probably be on there too.

If you're going to work with non-actors, get them to put something (or do it yourself) onto tape. This can be a speech or a joke or a bit about themselves – anything that'll help you if you're sitting at home scriptwriting or rewriting. Non-actors are exactly that, and they will be bringing their own personalities to their role rather than professionally creating new ones. To bring out the believable in your characters using amateurs, give them something that's at least within their own spectrum.

If you're not sure about your actors and their rapport, put them through a scene together. In fact, feel free to put them through the toughest bootcamp scene you've got. Consider yourself the sacrificial lamb in this exercise, as any bonding will be done between them at your own directorial expense.

ownership and exploitation. At the very least, you should have full rights to using your actors' performance as your own and however you will. Your actors should have no claim over how their image is used or any other part of the movie, inclusive of profits. It's a harsh world.

Finding the Crew

Crew? What crew? Surely there's just you and your camera and your actors? Well, maybe, but if that's the case then you are going to find yourself far too busy to actually shoot anything. If you want to get anywhere near collecting all the shots you need to put a movie together in the edit, you'll need a crew.

You might have got this far with just yourself or with a group of the like-minded. Therefore the problems are either where to find clones of yourself, or how to make your buddies do everything you tell them. Neither of these will happen. To find the like-minded, there are plenty of websites, colleges and forums that have a whole host of wannabes and wannados. If you're aiming to write and direct, you'll want the wannados.

Some people are very good at being told what to do. Those who think their ideas are better are not so good. If you've got this far, though, you're pretty determined to see your own idea through, and establishing control and an invisible hierarchy will take it through the shoot. At minimum, you'll need another person who will respond quickly to demand. It's not ideal, but it will help. What you could really do with, however, is a camera operator, a sound operator and a runner (an all-purpose assistant).

If you are aiming to be the director of your movie, though, you may want to wield the camera yourself. While this means framing the shots exactly how you want them, it doesn't mean that you will get all the shots that you want, or the performances, or the sound, or the stills. Most individuals can only do one thing at one time, and when the pressure's on on the set, even that one thing becomes a huge task and responsibility.

If this all sounds impossible, it's not. The best thing to do is to look at your movie and see what it requires and then allocate tasks. The most sensible way of breaking down a minimum crew, based on talent and time on set is:

- Director
- Camera and sound
- Set-dresser, lighting and effects
- Hair, make-up, make-up effects, props and wardrobe
- Production co-ordinater, shotlister and runner
- Production stills photographer

If there are fewer co-ordinators than six of you, then try not to skimp on any of the roles. Just try to work it somehow so that all bases are covered. Really, your actors probably don't know yet how adept they are at applying their own make-up, let alone taking a couple of pictures or holding a mic themselves. The fact is that effective results in audio and visuals are not rocket science, no matter the mystique in which professionals like to veil their trade. Learning new skills is all part of making yourself indispensable in the future. The way to try and engineer it is not to let lighting, say, take up your valuable directing time, but to relate all your lighting set-ups to you as a director – which is going to make you a better visual director.

The process of movie-making is not without its frustrations, tempers and creative anguish. It certainly ain't no picnic unless you've got a team of people who understand some kind of hierarchy and are willing to help whenever they are asked to. Spot-on initiative is really what you need in your crew. But whatever your mucking-in regime, make sure that it's reasonably co-ordinated. The last thing you want is to find you've lost your audio because your lighting expert's gone to get a round of cappuccinos.

One last thing about having someone taking stills: you might think screen grabs in the edit will do the trick, but once these are de-interlaced you're going to have half the amount of pixels of a digital 500,000-pixel video image – which is far lower than the four million pixels of the average digital stills camera. If you are thinking of publicizing your movie in the press, get high-resolution stills from a proper digital camera. It's the only way your movie will shine on the printed page.

One thing about female actors is that they are good at putting on their own make-up. This is only a time-saving blessing when you've discussed exactly what you want in the character and on your talent's face.

It's a good thing if one of your runners is hanging around. It means that they are there. If there isn't anything to do at a certain moment,

don't get rid of them on some spurious errand – you can guarantee that they won't be there when you really need them.

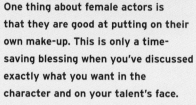

If you've got the luxury of a sound op, make sure that you've got the equipment to make them worthwhile. Audio will be half your battle if you're going to get the movie that you want, and having a boom in a bare room will help you get the best from your dialogue.

Art Department

Hollywood movies are all about creating an illusion, and it takes a lot of people to make the illusion look real. Sets full of actors don't become scenes until they have the right look, and getting that look is an art.

During preproduction, the art department for a movie is generally considered a low priority until production begins. Until your movie actually starts shooting, it's easier to worry about budgets, locations, actors, gear – the big guys. Don't. Try and find the time to make way for the one area of your movie that is going to make it a movie and not a fly-on-the-wall, back-garden production.

Usually, the best way of dealing with make-up, wardrobe, props and effects is to leave at least one person in charge of them. Fully briefed on the movie, the themes, the storyboard and the shooting schedule, they should be armed with all the actors' numbers and a budget of some description. Don't be cheap when you're putting it together: this is where your movie gloss can shine.

MAKE-UP

Everybody wears make-up in a movie – even if it doesn't look as though they do. In some cases, the audience is not meant to notice it, while in others it absolutely should. The audience doesn't want to look at spots and blemishes in a romantic comedy – but if characters have

them, they will have been made up to have them by design.

Let your art department use their imagination. They might even come up with ideas that you haven't considered that work with your themes. Claire Higgins' character, Julia, in the horror film *Hellraiser*, was designed to have gradually more arched and poisonous-coloured eyeshadows and lipstick shades as her scenes progressed. Make-up can assist progress in your characters – even if you have nothing more than a simple ugly-duckling storyline.

Choose your basics – and ask your actors to bring their own selection, if they have them. Meet the actors before you begin buying, to tailor to their skin. A dark and light powder foundation with a good thick application brush is essential to counteract sweat and reflection from hot lights. A white eyeliner is always useful for widening eyes in long shots. Lipsticks, blushers and eyeshadow shades are discretionary, but do remember to get an eyebrow brush for close-ups.

Even after thousands of years of evolution, some men are still afraid of make-up. Don't let them be. No matter what your actor might say (usually through inexperience), make-up is there to make them look

The inexperienced male actor might tell you that he doesn't need make-up, but your camera will tell you otherwise. Foundation and an eyebrow brush can be necessary evils.

better and look the part. Male actors usually require slightly darker foundations than their female equivalents. Don't forget their eyebrows; and let them know well before the shoot whether they should arrive shaven or unshaven.

Does your talent look good? It's time to make them look bad. If you want them to sweat, don't just stick the actor under lights. Dabbing glycerine with a cotton bud will do the trick, but make sure it's the last thing you apply. It's sticky, and any make-up on top just congeals. If you're on location, try and carry some spray-gun water and a flannel, as well as make-up remover in case you have to start from scratch.

You might want to make your characters sweat, but you shouldn't do the same to your actors. Some well-applied glycerine will look more realistic than the real thing.

WARDROBE

Like make-up, the wardrobe of the actors defines their characters: in Hollywood, clothes maketh the man. Usually, you won't want to work against this, but occasionally you might. If a character is uncomfortable in a situation, find something that makes them stand out, or is too tight around the collar. If they are going to die, or they're in a crowd and you want them to stand out, put them in red. If they're in a funk, put them in blue. These are thematic decisions. Work with the storyboard for your wardrobe. There's no point in trying to find the most outrageous shoes that you can lay claim to if the scene

is full of closed-frame medium shots and close-ups. Similarly, you won't want to give your actors revealing outfits if the scene is being shot from the floor.

The bottom line with wardrobe is to be realistic, both practically and cinematically. Practically, there isn't the budget to buy fabulous outfits for everybody; cinematically, it's not going to be believable if you do. Actors need to be comfortable in what they're wearing because it's one thing off their mind when they're acting. Give them a character spec alongside a breakdown of their scenes and get them to bring along mix-and-match clothes that work with those ideas. In short, you might not be able to clothe your gangsters in Armani suits or put your female lead in a Gucci dress, but you can do better than Michael Douglas' sweater in *Basic Instinct*'s club scene.

PROPS

As discussed, props can also help define your character. Some actors make use of practical props at hand, some bring their own if they truly understand the character, but most of them you'll have to find yourself. Some props are there to create the believability factor in your set. Others are metaphoric character or theme extensions, while others are simply plot devices.

If you've a McGuffin, you don't necessarily have to be specific. One hands-on prop can stand in as well as one hard-to-find prop. You can easily go overboard on metaphors, too. While some directors will wax lyrical about how an ornament on the wall describes the protagonist's inner turmoil, there are far better ways to spend your time and energy than on this sort of thing.

Think of the cutaway to a rubber Mickey Mouse during *An American Werewolf in London*'s transformation scene. It's ironic, it talks about real bestial pain and mockery, it's cinematically self-referential and even better, it refers to the ridiculous cutaways used to hide the joins in old-fashioned Hollywood werewolf transformations – something that the groundbreaking sequence laughs in the face of.

the shoot

Introduction

If it's the first day of your first shoot, you may be excited or you may find it's the first day of snowballing panic. To ensure that it isn't a race against time, treat it like an exam. Prep before you go to bed.

Your batteries should be on charge and everything else packed and ready to go. Your checklist goes something like this:

→ Storyboard
→ Shooting schedule
→ More scripts than you need
→ Digital video camera
→ DV batteries
→ More DV tape than you need
→ Tripod/stabilizer
→ (Digital) stills camera with enough memory or film
→ Mics/boom
→ Spare mic batteries
→ Lights
→ Spare bulbs
→ Gels
→ Reflectors
→ Make-up
→ Wardrobe
→ Props
→ Cash

Sound a lot? It's the bare minimum.

Your job for the day from then on is just to keep cool. There are no problems; there are only challenges – and on the day, it's time that is your biggest adversary.

The point about time is that it takes a very special director and producer to understand the theory of relativity in your shoot. Time flies when you're filming, and seems to get as much compressed during the shoot as any transition will make it when you're cutting the film together. Worse still, time is spent doing all the fussy things that either could have been done before or that have no bearing on the movie itself.

This is where you need to be focussed. The point of the shoot is that you're trying to get all the shots and audio that are on your shooting schedule. Any extra time spent should be dedicated to upping the production values of what the audience will see.

For every set-up, you need to remember:

→ White balance
→ Exposure (zebra stripes)
→ Shutter speed (refer to exposure)
→ Sound check
→ Preroll (bars and tone for start of tapes)
→ Action

Good housekeeping on set will always save you time. Carry a spare tape in your pocket. Flick the Save button of every tape you use. Don't

Storyboards, contact numbers, scripts, mobile phone, release forms... with so much to remember you need to get it all ready and charged to go.

record onto the last two minutes or the first two minutes of every tape. Label tapes and boxes before and detail them after you've used them. Start a different roll number in the timecode for each tape. Always shoot at least one more take for safety. You can't assume you've got it right first time, and it gives you one more option in the edit. To give yourself a chance, consider these potential problems with every take:

LIGHTS

→ Are all the non-practical lights out of camera safety area?

→ Is any unwanted shadow being cast during action?

→ Is anything so close that it will burn?

CAMERA

→ Is the lens clean?

→ Are you set to the right ratio?

→ Have you made sure that the date isn't being printed in-frame?

→ Are your exposure, zoom and focus set to automatic?

AUDIO

→ Is there any hum, hiss or feedback from cross-frequencies or magnetic proximity?

→ Is there any noise from lavaliers against fabric or jewellery?

→ Has the mic level been adjusted?

If all these are checked and your schedule's realistic, you'll be well on your way with at least a little confidence. And it is a confidence trick. Whether you feel odd or not, shouting 'rolling...and...*action'*, as well as '...and cut', is part of the job. Convincing your actors and crew that you are serious, that time is marching on and that you know what you are doing is the trick to creating the illusion.

60 Hot Shots

Hollywood movies are all about communicating with an audience, telling them the story through the distribution of a controlled stream of information. This information can be overt, obscure or anywhere in between, and the information itself is comprised of words, music and shots. These three elements can be withheld or released to allow the story to be told at the filmmaker's pace.

THE LONG SHOT

THE ESTABLISHER

The reason that shots are so vital to the distribution of information is that they control what the viewer is allowed to see and what they are not. The audience is being given a window onto the movie's world and everything must take place there in order to make sense of a story. Therefore everything within that frame must be clear and visible.

It's one thing getting all the shots you need in some kind of order to tell that story; it's another to make sure that the audience can see what you're trying to show them. The types of framing of a shot, therefore, are important to understand.

This is a wide shot that shows an audience the world you are placing your story in, describing the location without necessarily showing or disguising anything vital. This relieves the audience of having to do any guesswork as to where the scene is set or where the characters are situated. Establishers are usually found at the beginning of a movie to locate the setting without clumsy exposition (New York in *Fatal Attraction*) – or, if fictional, let the audience in on an unknown world (the cityscape of *Blade Runner*). They ease the audience into a movie or a new location within it.

The long shot (LS) is a small establisher. The language of movies has changed with the sophistication of audiences – once the long shot came at the top of every different scene – and even now it works to locate the characters of your movie in a small corner of the world shown in the establishing shot. This works with an audience in exactly the same way as the establisher, reassuring them that they are not being deceived. This is where we are, these are the characters that we're interested in, and this is the physical order of the characters in their environment. This last point is important, as it explains how characters react to each other's position in tighter shots.

THE MEDIUM SHOT

The medium shot (MS) shifts the emphasis from location to character. It informs us of how they're dressed, what they're doing and how they physically respond to each other. For these reasons, it can give a lot more away as to body language between characters and action within the location. Body language and actions are signatures of dialogue and can be translated to read as remark or response, which is why medium shots are often used sparingly to accompany dialogue. The close-up (CU) is the standard

THE CLOSE-UP

form for dialogue, framing the whole of the head and shoulders of the actor. It's a convention and relies on the MS and LS to put the eyeline and direction of conversation in context. CUs are also convention for significant props and can be used to emphasize irony (the rubber Mickey Mouse in *An American Werewolf in London*'s transformation scene) or give clues to an audience (Dan putting the kitchen knife down in *Fatal Attraction* is the residue of the original framed-for-murder ending).

THE CUTAWAY

A CU is often a cutaway that heals any jump-cut wounds. Cutaways are shots of 'nothing in particular' that carry dialogue over the top to make an easy-on-the-eye – or ear – transition from what might otherwise have been a jarring cut.

A series of edited CUs used without an MS or an LS serves to take your subject out of context. This is called Fragmentation, and turns each shot into part of a jigsaw puzzle of the subject. By not showing the full picture to an audience, you can either frustrate them or cleverly manipulate them. The CU as fragmentation is often used as a montage to create the effect of a full picture – this is montage. The effect of this is either to fetishize the image or condense time (in a jump-cut). Because it compresses time, fragmentation can be used to get rid of those tedious essentials in movies and turn them into punctuation (Jamie Lee Curtis and Bruce Campbell dressing in *Blue Steel* and *Evil Dead II*).

THE EXTREME CLOSE-UP

An extreme close-up (XCU) is anything tighter than a CU and is the ultimate in labouring on detail. If it's used on an actor, it's also a test of your make-up artist's skills. Because of its disarming and unusually employed intimacy – especially on the big screen – it's either used for visual effect, or to draw an audience's attention to something a character has or hasn't seen. XCUs are often used for eyes in order to startle an audience right back (*The Texas Chainsaw Massacre*). If it's used on a prop, it might well be evidence in a thriller (the raised typewriter 't' in *Jagged Edge*), or as an unseen omen or metaphor in an arthouse movie (the ant-infested ear in *Blue Velvet*).

Between all of these shots are variant mid-ranges, with different effects on location, character or detail. The combination of all of these shots creates a rhythm that makes your scenes easier to cut and more palatable to watch.

Framing the Shot

Maintaining order within chaos while shooting is a learned skill, while disorder tends to manifest itself in grabbing shots where you can towards the end of the day. The best way to maintain control is by constant reference to your shooting schedule for time and budget – and to your storyboard for production values and the final edit.

Controlling your shots is often best done at storyboard stage. Previsualization using thorough pre-production research (locations, props, actors, themes et al) will mean that you know exactly how you want the shots to work in the edit, and how they have to be composed on set.

This deliberate composition is termed *mise-en-scène*, and while it sounds like it's going to waste even more time on the set, it won't. The reason is that once the work has been done at storyboard stage, you'll know exactly what you want when you shoot. In any case, time spent on *mise-en-scene* is never wasted. If you ever thought that there was something undeniably cool about the look of *Fight Club*, *The Matrix* or *The Hulk*, then it's not just to do with hulking budgets (though these certainly help) – it's to do with *mise-en-scène*.

Mise-en-scène covers both what's in the frame – locations, sets, props, costumes, lighting – but also the way that it's shot: framing, focus and camera movement. It's all about aesthetics, a field which has been with us since art began.

If you can get your composition working with the *mise-en-scène* in frame and the movement of the camera, you create something that's as carefully choreographed as a ballet, but with the advantage that you can make it flow even better in the edit. Once you get there, you can use cuts and transitions to hide information or add tension, build a rhythm, or just smooth over the joins. With storyboarded transitions, it's important that not only is the audience following the action during a distracting transition, but that the move from one scene to another using an effect works with both scenes. This kind of complexity takes an artist, a design engineer and an experienced director.

Bah, humbug. You can be as experienced as the best of them. Imagination is free, camera moves can be planned and transitions experimented with. Try a few out during preproduction and you'll be a lot more confident later. That way, you can save even more time when it comes to the shoot. Also think about whether formal or informal compositions are best suited to your time, budget, genre and scene.

A long shot with characters on a horizon, accompanied by looped audio. The Hollywood way at this distance is to keep the camera locked-off on a tripod and let them walk through the frame. The aesthetic convention continues - usually - to cut before they have left the frame, and not leave a pregnant retina-burning image of a no-scape with the audience.

Look for the geometrics of your scene and work them in a way that they guide the eye. Eyes follow arrow shapes by default, and perspective to a visible or invisible vanishing point creates natural guidelines. What this often allows you to do is to move your action away from being centre-frame, something that can add dynamism to your shots.

Cutting through a frame to create one-third/two-thirds is part of the Golden Section rule. If you want to maintain this, it's either up to your direction of your actors, your camera op – or simply to put a physical barrier into the frame, which automatically stops your talent from intruding into your aesthetic setup.

Think about your edit as you roll. Shooting wider on a long shot permits more space for a more aesthetic and meaningful transition. Here, the medium shot of the two actors follow the lines of the long shot through the mix, emphasizing their conflict with the rigid division that the clash of landscapes creates.

THE ART OF COMPOSITION

Psychological studies have proven that some compositions are simply more pleasing to the eye. The Golden Section is one of these. The Greeks broke down a two-dimensional scene into one-third/two-third sections, which transformed in the movies into the division of the frame into nine equal parts. The points of intersection of the lines are the important parts, and those to which the eye is drawn.

Great moviemakers have learned that they can use the Golden Section to train or deceive the eye. Indeed, horror movies rely on it, asking the audience to look at one part of the frame, then surprising them in another. Using diagonals also forces the eye to look at one point of the image.

Moving Pictures

Movies are not just moving because the actors are moving, but because the camera is moving. The camera has to be the audience's eye: if you just stick with a fixed position, then your film becomes nothing more than theatre on video. Learn how to use camera movement, and you can learn how to show what you want to show and hide what you want to hide from your audience. And once you can do that, you have them in your power.

But, as *Spider-Man* was told, with great power comes great responsibility. You have to use your moves to excite, entertain, thrill, deceive and put your audience right where you need them to be emotionally and physically.

With every framed shot, there are three main options for moving your camera. All of these are best performed with a tripod.

Zoom

This is a move in to your subject without the camera op moving physically forwards. It's the most overused feature of a DV camcorder, and for maximum misuse should be undertaken with a last gasp wobble to try and relocate the subject while manhandling the zoom control.

In fact, there's even a way to make it worse: use the digital zoom. No matter how much your camera might trumpet its digital zoom, turn it off in the camera's setup menu. As we covered on page 17, all it does is take the maximum optical zoom and blow up the pixels until you can't recognize anything.

Zooms are not often used in Hollywood movies, as getting closer to the subject is usually best done with a cut or by tracking into the shot. When zooms are used, however, they are used to hammer home a point. Think of the crash zooms in *Exorcist III*'s hospital scene or even those deliberately used badly by the 'camcorder' in *Signs*. These are both carefully contrived as punctuation shock scenes. Any other use of zooms is likely to be a very gentle push in to a subject, and should be hardly noticeable in its degree or speed.

Pan

This is a horizontal move from left to right, or from right to left, without moving the camera on its axis. 'Pan' is probably the most bastardized term in digital video, and the way it's used always separates the amateurs from the pros. It's not a tracking shot (the camera rotates but doesn't move) and it's not a tilt.

A pan is used a lot in Hollywood movies to get from one subject to another. Used as a close-up, it can take us from one actor to another in conversation; as a medium shot, it can take us from one group of actors to another in situation.

Pans can be used with speed to effect in-camera transitions (a whip pan off the end of the first scene cut against a whip pan into the start of the second scene), or you can pull focus from one part of the scene to another to change its emphasis from left to right and also front to back.

Tilt

A tilt is a vertical move from up to down, or from down to up – again without moving the camera's axis. It works exactly the same as a pan, just on a vertical plane. Because of the 4:3 or 16:9 ratio, pans tend to be used more than tilts in movies. They're more effective, aesthetically speaking – to work with the frame – and gravity has a way of making most things in life work on the horizontal rather than the vertical.

As a long shot, a tilt can take us from sky to landscape or the door of a skyscraper to the fifteenth floor. As a medium shot, it can stay with a character moving towards a low-positioned camera, and as a tight it can follow a character's eyes down to a noticed prop.

These three moves are the basics, and as such, they can be combined. A zoom with a tilt, therefore, takes us from our hero bursting in through the lobby door to the silhouetted fracas in a room on the fifteenth floor that he is racing to get to. While tripods allow all of these moves to take place without much fudging, they still have an inherent

A tracking shot in Hollywood is a camera on a mount - a dolly - running on tracks. With DV, you can get away with a car, a shopping cart or even a skateboard to take your camera from your point A to your point B.

The POV shot is usually undertaken handheld, at camera op height, and without specifically settling on any particular thing for long. It's an emulation of the human eye - but not a true one. Accept it as part of the 'reality DV' language. The human eye works more gyroscopically, with the brain making adjustments. A digital video camera using an Optical Image Stabilizer can recreate this effect, which is why a handheld MiniDV with all of its baggage of personal, physical viewpoint, is ideal for POV shots.

rigidity that might make the shot pass by comprehensively, but not always emotionally.

In order to involve an audience, the camera ops themselves must move. If the lens is the audience's eye, taking the lens into the action and giving it a motion and perspective that relates to the human experience implicates the audience. This is never truer than with the POV (Point of View) shot. Instead of taking a spectator into the scene itself, this takes us behind the eyes of an individual and indicates what they are viewing or participating in. *Halloween* is the masterclass here, the opening sequence looking through the eyeholes of young

Michael Myers' mask and enclosing the audience with suitably muffled atmos and over-amped breathing.

Remember: a camera move is transitional. It takes us from one place to another for a reason. If there isn't a reason, it's just padding – and if the point of your movie is the story, then there's just no space for padding. Unless you're Brian DePalma or Dario Argento, a virtuoso camera move merely brings everything to a standstill. A to B usually means going from wide scene to tight character shot or following a character through a location. If you're doing either, it might be best accomplished with a tracking shot.

In Hollywood, a tracking shot involves a camera on a mount – a dolly – running on tracks. With DV, you won't need heavy industrial dollies for tracking shots. Instead, you can use anything from cars to skateboards to take the camera from your A to your B. There are three main factors to success here: the smoothness of the surface, the suspension of the wheels and the fixing of the camera. Once you've got that in mind, it's all down to DIY practicality: vinyl tiles on concrete, rubber bands around wheels, cut-off rubber glove arms as strapping.

The next challenge, of course, is to stay in control of the camera while it's in motion.

66 Taking Control

Controlling the image is the name of the game when it comes to recreating the look of the Hollywood movie. Using auto-anything on a camera can undermine that control and cause you to make judgments that are compromised. Turn them all off and have your own way with depth of field, shutter speed and exposure.

Light means everything to a digital video camera. The analogue world is lit naturally and artificially to create form and depth. These are the things that need to be captured. Your DV camera's shutter is not the same as a traditional film camera, which uses a gate that physically opens and closes for a certain amount of time to expose light onto light-sensitive celluloid for that given instant. Because you've a CCD (or three) instead of film, the 'shutter speed' is really the duration that each frame is allowed to sample the image onto the CCD.

The relationship that this has with your actual f-stop exposure setting is that – absolutely like a film camera – the exposure setting controls the amount of light that you're letting in for each of those CCD image samples. Therefore, the greater the amount of light, the quicker your 'shutter speed' can be while maintaining a visible image. The slower the duration of shutter speed, the less light is actually required.

This logic is preprogrammed in any automatic setting that you might have. A 'running man' icon, for instance, means the shutter speed is set to take a sample of the image every $\frac{1}{10,000}$th of a second. This realtime value is different for PAL and NTSC as they are always recording at, respectively, 25 frames (50 fields) every second and 30 frames (60 fields every second). Because each sample is so quick, the light has to be bright enough to define the image. Therefore the exposure setting compensates (widens) to let more light in.

With low shutter speeds ($\frac{1}{30}$), the image is allowed to be pretty dark because of the longer duration of the sampled image. What this means, though, is that there is more chance of movement within the frame for that duration, which creates a blur in each frame. Conversely, the quick samples for 'running man' are so that the action can be viewed as a series of short 'snapshots'. This gives a noticeably animated feel to fast motion with a fast shutter speed.

So, while automatic settings will let you shoot anything you want within parameters, you can only get full control over your image once you've understood the logic and done some experimentation. As you're contriving the light and image that you're shooting, you've got a far better chance of getting exactly what you want. Think back to the hyper-real fast shutter-speed attacks in *28 Days Later*. In low light, the way to do it – and to actually witness the image – is to light the whole scene way beyond what you might think is reasonable on the set. In other words, it's gonna get hot in there!

This animated effect is precisely what differentiates the look of video and the look of film. *Jurassic Park*'s CGI effects made the imported digital images compatible with the surrounding film environment by adding a slight blur to the movement within each graphic frame. If you want a more filmic look to your Hollywood movie, then a lower shutter speed will help. This is just one of the elements to that effect, which will be discussed later.

This juggling act between amount of light and duration of image sample also affects your focus. A high f-stop exposure, letting in a lot of light, brings everything in the frame closer to being in focus with your subject. This serves to flatten the entire image. Depth of field – something that film is very capable of – is created by 'stopping down'. This means going down to a low f-stop exposure, particularly when you've got a brightly lit image. With a medium or tight camera angle and a low f-stop, you can create a depth of field significant enough to pull focus between two subjects. The balance is, of course, that the bright image that you might have dictates that the

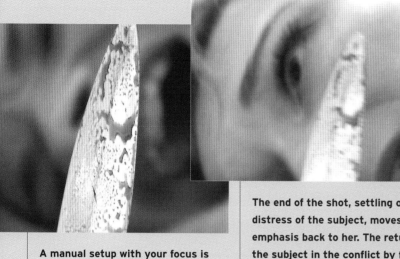

A manual setup with your focus is going to allow you to rack between shots. If you've got a well-lit set, this will let you work with your focus better to get those shots that you want. It's not an arbitrary business – to get the effect of drama, suspense or horror, the use of focus is integral. With this shot, focussing on the knife gives it importance in the frame and tells us that it has intruded without actually showing what it has done.

The end of the shot, settling on the distress of the subject, moves the emphasis back to her. The return to the subject in the conflict by focus (the knife, after all, is just the obstacle), can then continue her progression in the scene.

A slow shutter speed at a high exposure on a well-lit set will make your shot unworkable. If you're looking for an effected shutter speed shot on such a set, take the exposure down to avoid burning out the frame.

shutter speed is a faster setting, and therefore the effects of your attractive film-like blur could be minimized.

Just as automatic camera settings compromise on light and speed, you'll have to, too. Bear in mind, though, that as the director, you can dictate the amount of light in the frame and the speed of the action in the frame. These used with enough camera know-how can at least get you less of a compromise and more of the look that you actually want.

This particular scene has very little light. Worse still, the medium shot and depth of field won't allow for the 'killer' to be knocked back out of focus, the original design for the shot.

In situations like this, the use of a 'flickering television' (see page 172) helps with the same effect, the killer appearing and disappearing in darkness behind the victim.

Lighting

Whatever you're shooting, let there be light.

There's light everywhere and it can all be used somehow. All that you need to understand from the start is that different types of light – particularly artificial light – don't always behave in the same way.

There are essentially two different types of bulb. A bulb with a filament source (an incandescent lamp) creates light by passing a current through a wire, just as you might see in a domestic lightbulb. A bulb with an arc source creates light from a space between two electrodes. A still shot of an overhead fluorescent striplight demonstrates this 'lightning bolt' effect. This light, though, is not emitted from the arc itself, but from electrons passing through the phosphor-coated tube and producing light-emitting photons.

Within these two types, there are different ways of either coating the filament or making up the phosphor, creating different wavelengths of light within the spectrum. These variations affect the colour of the light source – colour temperature – something we measure in degrees Kelvin. The lower the measure in degrees, the redder the colour – right down to infrared; the higher the measure, the bluer the light will be – right up to ultraviolet.

Light is created through heat, and the reason that tungsten tends to be used in a filament bulb is that it has the highest melting temperature of all known materials (3,680°K). The sun at its height is around 6,000°K, making it impossible to represent with a filament bulb. A domestic 60W bulb, measured at 2,500°K, will warm up environments and subjects with a reddish light, but comes nowhere close to representing daylight. A domestic halogen lamp might measure up to 3,600°K, bringing it closer to the cooler blue of natural sunlight.

Colour temperature comes from the source itself; the actual colour of the light is seen by reflection in everything within the shot. Every object and subject reflects different colours of light to a different degree depending on the surface. This is what the white balance control on your DV camera is for: to shoot true to your set, you push the white balance with the lens focussed on a white surface under the lighting.

While shooting clean – that is, without any effects or 'creative' settings – is always recommended, check that your edit software allows for colour correction. If it doesn't, you don't have the right lights on set, and you want a different effect (redder or bluer), take the camera elsewhere to get a white balance under different lights and bring it back to the set on standby.

Okay, so that's the science part: where do the lights go? Three-point lighting is the classic lighting setup, and it provides a solid basis to illuminate your set and subject solidly. Once you have that down correctly, you can start to play around with variations.

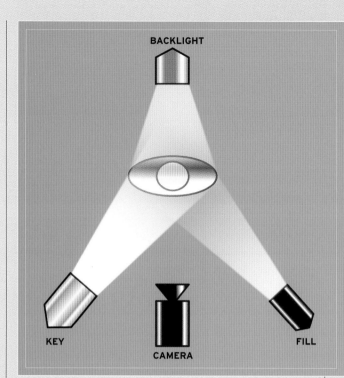

THREE-POINT LIGHTING

Key
Does what it says on the label. It's the one light that lights up your subject.

Fill
This light is the one that eliminates any harsh shadows that the key creates, and it's usually placed at about 90 degrees to the key.

Backlight
This lights from the back in order to create more of an edge around the subject and pull them away from the background.

If you can beg, borrow or rent professional lighting, this is probably what you will be using. A redhead is termed an 'open-faced luminaire' but all this really means is that it has no lens system. Redheads are usually 800-1000W and a highly efficient means of colour-corrected light as a small portable mains unit.

If your light is an open-face (a plain lamp with no shields or focusing assemblies), barndoors come to the rescue. Without a lens to focus the light, you need them to shield light from the places that you would rather have in shadow.

70 More on Light

Three-point lighting is a convention – but that doesn't mean to say that it has to be conventional. Varying the type of light, the colour of light, the strength of light and the position of light can change the entire look of your scene – for better or for worse. Adding just one more light can transform a well-lit set into one that kicks butt. Again, you might need to buy, borrow or rent one of these, but if you're shooting on a set then the results are worth your while.

Spots

Spots are smaller, focusable incandescents. They're usually termed fresnels, which refers to the convex lens with concentric ridges that reduce heat and weight. Fresnels are the kind of thing that you might find above your head at a rock gig, and they do a fantastic job at pinpointing or flooding light within a specific spot.

Eyelights

Eyelights can be created with tight or barn-doored spots, aimed to give sparkle to your talent's eyes. They can give them a soul, help emote, sex them up or pick up tears. Conversely, they can be used to implicate robots (*Westworld*) or the possessed (*The Second Coming*).

Kickers

Kickers accentuate a particular area of background interest: they work to up the aesthetic values or meaning of your shots.

There are also a few other things that can be added to make your lights work harder for you:

Coloured gels

By putting these coloured polyester sheets over your lights, you can create other moods or emulate computer or television screens (blue). Extreme colours (red and green) can give you madness, funhouse or religious effects and the more subdued examples can lift your scene to be sunnier (yellow), stormier or duskier (indigo). The one thing to always watch out for when dropping anything in front of a light is that it doesn't burn. 'What's that smell?' is said as often as 'cut' on badly managed sets.

Gobos

A gobo is nothing more complicated than a fabric or wood shape placed in front of a light to create a particular shadow. Gobos can be created just by cutting out cardboard shapes (crosses, window frames or whatever) and installing them in front of the light source. To make sure that your shapes don't diffuse much (unless you actually want them to) use a spotlight that you can focus manually.

Scrims

Scrims are fine meshes that diffuse the light and any harsh outlines that they create. While you can use fabrics from around the home, just remember that they need to be kept at a safe distance from the hot light. They can also be opaque gels that can add a pleasing and natural softness to faces and entire sets.

Reflectors and deflectors

Reflecting light on – and deflecting light off – the subjects and set can add to the attraction and lose the distraction from your shot. Painting foil with diluted acrylic creates a surface that's perfect for bouncing light without dazzling the lens or your talent.

While arranging your lights, the most important thing to remember is that light means nothing to a CCD or

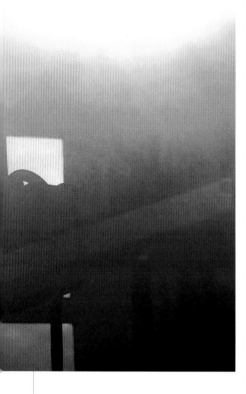

Manufacturers like Lowel and Ionero make families of reflectors and diffusers, and if you're going to buy into them, you won't have much change left to make your movie. All of these, though, are rentable: available down at your local disco-lighting store for daily rates.

three without shadow. The contrast between your blacks and highlights, and the mid-tones in between, ensure that form is seen. Digital video, though, especially when compressed to a DVD-friendly MPEG format, has a way of revealing artefacts in movement, crushing blacks and losing detail in highlights when there is a huge contrast. On some high-end cameras you can check for anything that will scream at you later by flicking over to your zebra setting. What this does is warn you of any areas of your picture that could be problematic with zebra stripes.

Remember that using a powerful editing package will give you some more options later. If you want to up the levels of contrast in your image, you can usually alter them at the editing stage.

When a light becomes a luminaire, it means that all the mechanical fixings and the lens optics are incorporated into the light. This is the Vari-Lite 2416, which offers intensity control and strobing. If you manage to get a theatrical space to work in, this is the kind of wash luminaire that you may be lucky enough to find pre-installed.

A couple of 500W halogen lamps can efficiently flood your set and warm up your shots. These are cheapest when bought from DIY shops, and will come complete with positioning mounts.

Sound Advice

Quiet on set. No, really – your audio is the most precious thing that you're eventually going to have to work with, and your camera mic (being ultra-efficient) is going to pick up everything that you don't want.

A DV camera mic's pick-up range is cardioid and takes sound from a shape like this (below):

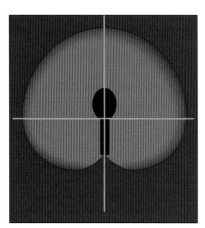

That means that although you're aiming your fixed mic in the direction of your action, you're still picking up audio from 360 degrees around the mic with a minimum level towards yourself as operator.

A camera mic on a closed set is worse – especially in a hard, unfurnished room. Not only does it make every sound on set audible, but exaggerated and subject to a cold hollow echo.

This is precisely the reason why audio booths in postproduction facilities are furnished vacuums. They dull every incidental sound and use a directional mic such as a hyper or supercardioid.

A super or hypercardioid has a more directional pick-up range, which looks like this:

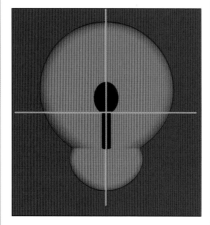

Why is clear audio such an issue in a visual medium? Well, the language of cinema does not incorporate different levels of audio quality. Even in hyper-real DV movies like *The Blair Witch Project*, distorted, overblown or hissy audio is one thing audiences won't tolerate. The plus side of this is that good audio will gloss over some of your least favourite shots without a hitch. So what do you have to do to get it?

Shoot clean is the answer. And 'clean' with audio means not only quiet on set and getting the mic away from the noisy parts of your camera, but getting all your audio elements separately, if you can.

Look to your edit software for answers. Hopefully, it will allow for a few audio tracks. What this means is that those separate elements of audio can be layered and given levels to create the exact sound and ambience that you need for each scene. Ideally, your edit software (or any other audio software that you might have) will have filters of its own. These filters – or gates – let more bass or more treble through and allow for your audio to be warmer or colder. They can use these filters to clean up any hum or hiss that you might end up with.

In an edit, audio is often layered as dialogue, sound effects, atmos, Voice Of God (voice-over) and music: five basic tracks. When you're shooting, dialogue is the most important, so try turning off the camera mic and using lavaliers (collar microphones) to get it straight. Check the volume levels in the camera to make sure that you're not peaking, as any audio for DV that is over 0 decibels will either sound horrific or not even register. Make sure you're wearing your headphones for this.

When recording dialogue, the shots will dictate the kind of mic set-up that you're going to use. External mics can – and have to – be hidden, whether behind a prop in the frame, or just out of frame. A wide, long or travelling shot with sync sound is best handled with wireless lavaliers. If you're shooting tighter than this, disguise the mics in the clothing or jewellery of your talent, making sure that they don't pick up any incidental rustling.

If your shot is too tight to get away with lavaliers (a medium to loose close-up), then get some assistance and use an external mic just out of frame. If this is below the actors, the sound tends to be more bassy, as it picks up reverberations from the chest and throat of your actors. If the mic's held, fixed or hanging above them, you'll get a more balanced tone to your audio.

When you're checking back your pictures, always check for your audio as well, with the same headphones. Looping dialogue in an edit is not the best fun to be had.

Dialogue, though, isn't everything. Dialogue in a vacuum is absolutely not real at all. There is always some noise everywhere, no matter what, and the professionals call this 'atmos'. Acceptable atmos to an audience doesn't include passing airplanes, revving cars, mooing cows or barking dogs unless it's part of the action. If there isn't an airplane, car, cow, dog, PA – or whatever – in shot, a few well-placed sound effects in the edit can enrich the location that your action is taking place in.

In order to get the atmos on location or set, just record a couple of minutes of natural ambience using the camera mic onto your tape. This is best done with your crew and talent off-set (to avoid idle chatter), and with your colour bars up (if you have them). This will help you identify the bit of tape when spooling through later. Introduce your atmos track vocally, clearly stating the scene and location, and you can't go too far wrong.

If you're attaching a lav to a lapel, make sure that you've got the right wardrobe and the right colour match. Leather is a good rigid way of concealing a mic...

...with just about the same sheen, if the camera catches it out.

Shooting Dialogue

Conversation is the driving force of the Hollywood movie. Dialogue reveals what characters think and know, what they did, do or what they're going to do. These are given to an audience through a series of statements, questions and answers. By turn, this exposes what they don't think, or know, and what they're not going to do, or what they haven't done. These elements incidentally create character traits. From here, personality is created by your talent. The dialogue in your script is reinterpreted and the effect becomes dependent on their timing and execution.

Dialogue is important – and if it's not, it shouldn't be there. While actions speak for themselves, delivered words require attention for comprehension. Because of this, dialogue is often given to an audience without too much flashy, discontinuous or illogical distraction.

Dialogue setups are gradually changing as the audience becomes more sophisticated. It used to be that distraction was avoided by creating the illusion of conversation within a closed frame. That is to say that the frame contained the conversation and the action, and the the dialogue shots were made up of variously angled MS cuts of the different characters, often alternating between them and without leaving a single environment.

One of most important parts of the classical Hollywood language is the 180-degree rule, heavily grounded in closed-frame shooting and editing. This is based on the conventional editing philosophy that smoothing

cuts from different angles within the same scene would avoid troubling an audience. In the 180-degree rule, an imaginary line runs through two

actors facing each other and any cut within that dialogue scene is taken from a shot on the same side. A cut from the other side of this line is regarded as a no-no, because it can result in a left-facing character

suddenly facing right (or vice versa), disorientating the audience.

In the right movie (that is, one that is hyper-real or one that wants to draw attention to the cuts) this rule can be broken. One way of breaking it without disorientation is by incorporating a move into the edit sequence that takes an audience with a dolly to the other side of the line so that cutting can start again. The point is that, again, it's one of those rules that you have to know before you can break it.

The rule is almost void when shooting conversation with three actors because the visual dynamics between your talent changes. This is all to do with their placement in the frame. If all your actors are facing each other, every character will be

adjacent to each of the other two characters. This fixes their position in a continuous circle and any breaking of the 180-degree rule will still be regarded with instant comprehension from the audience.

The only thing to really watch out for are straight cuts from one side of the same actor to their other side. Used as different POVs from the two remaining actors, though, it's an effect that can be used extremely inventively should you want to.

Closed-frame shooting also requires other elements to keep the scene believable and nondistracting. Eyelines are important, as they're the direction in which each character is looking. This isn't just vital in making postproduction effects look realistic, but equally important when shooting each character's medium and close-ups.

The growing preference in modern movies, though, is to use open frame for dialogue sequences. This is framing within a dialogue scene that allows for subjects or props or background devices to enter and exit the frame. It intimates a larger world outside the dialogue. While this is a more naturalistic way of shooting (it takes the characters out of the closed-frame bubble), it can also be more distracting or confusing for an audience.

The classic Hollywood movie is naturalistic and believable – but usually contrived. Creating a world that exists around your characters is not just a question of adding extras and props. In fact, there's a whole different practical side when shooting, such as lighting and avoiding shooting lights and cables, controlling background noise, and the nightmare of continuity – especially if your location is al fresco and your environment out of directorial control (if you're shooting

in a street, for instance). Unless it's a sight gag, may Hollywood forgive you if whatever is going on in your background is more entertaining than the conversation.

An open frame allows you to find different ways of creating natural transitions in frame. We'll discuss this later.

The other possible disruption to audience attention is a physical one: the mic. We've all seen it (and it's largely down to badly projected movies) and it's an issue of practicality. The problem is always how to get good audio without the mic being in shot. Lavaliers and boom placement have been touched on, but how does this work in a nonstatic shot?

Working with walking, talking actors presents its own challenges using a camera in motion. While your lavaliers may be prone to visual exposure (use coloured tape to disguise and adhere them), they can

also pick up wind (use little mufflers or tape on some cotton wool).

If you've got a boom and you're going to use it, the fun really starts. Walking backwards with it, avoiding the camera op and cables, keeping the whole thing out of shot while it gets heavier and heavier, is a good test for most audio ops. Being the director is no less of a trick, and you're best out of the way with monitor and headphones – it's all a bit pricey, though, in terms of time and money.

Closed frame? Open frame? Static? Motion? In the final analysis, it's the story that counts, and the dialogue drives the story. Doing whatever it takes to get that dialogue within the time available should be your biggest priority.

76 Louder than Words

If you've got an electric script that drives itself purely through dialogue and character, the writer will be David Mamet. If you don't, you'll need some action to keep your audience in their seats. Audiences get restless, which is why the Hollywood movie-pacing sine wave should look like an emotional, tense, horrific or hilarious rollercoaster.

The balance that creates this sine wave is often misunderstood. Dialogue is treated by bad Hollywood movies as the Achilles' heel – the low points – that the action high points must make up for. That's just shoddy writing. There is no reason at all why your movie should operate in turns of action, dialogue, action, dialogue, action.

With silent movies, the challenge was to put across the story, character and motivation without words. This is exactly how the action scene should work, complementing the dialogue and not just existing simply to adrenalize the story or give the characters something to talk about.

While dialogue scenes work better when started in the middle of a conversation, action scenes work better with a buildup. This helps them to integrate seamlessly into the story. They can be fight scenes, chase scenes or any other pivotal scenes that aren't dialogue-led, but they're usually all about conflict.

Action scenes that work, build. They start from quiet character moments and build either slowly or suddenly. Think of the build as tension, and the action as release.

The build

This is the continuation of your story. A character, whether established or not, continues their storyline into a scene that is the climax of that story arc. The only contradiction to this is a precredit intro, which may be the end of a fragmented arc explained or portrayed later on in the movie.

To create a build, there are three fundamental elements required: the protagonist, the antagonist and the location. Put together, these provide the situation. Mix them up and these things will eventually collide to give you the action.

Your protagonist is your main character. If they've already been established, an audience will second-guess how they respond to conflict, and any second-guessing by an audience can be manipulated into tension. The antagonist is your trump card – usually a character or characters who haven't been established so well. The antagonist doesn't have to be human: it can be an alien, a fire, a tornado, a dog, a shower of frogs. What matters is that he, she or it is there to be a force against your protagonist.

By rule of the Hollywood Happy Ending, the odds are always with your protagonist unless they are a peripheral or unpleasant character. By making your antagonist an unknown quantity or by handicapping your protagonist, tension can be maximized.

The build starts with the protagonist, armed with motivation, entering a location, sometimes hostile, effectively not. What the location and its inherent props can do, though, is anticipate the action, again creating tension. A dead-end, a dark attic, an empty street, a kitchen full of utensils, a parked car with keys, a roomful of corpses, flickering candles – all of these things, coupled with the situation (an investigation, an argument, an intrusion) add to the build that'll jump into...

The action

Once you get to the point of release, you need to maintain and crank up the tension until the scene reaches its natural conclusion. There are two ways of creating this tension. The first is with the story itself, and that involves the situation – the antagonist, protagonist and location. The second way is with the shots themselves.

The story is incidental here: it's whatever you've made it. The shots are pretty standard too. They're everything that you need to cut an action scene together.

An average Hollywood movie shot is somewhere between three and five seconds long. The average action shot, however, is somewhere between one and three seconds long. Therefore you need a lot of different angles to get the shots you need for your action scene.

Why so many and so short? Because this gives an illusion of dynamism. It involves the audience, giving them the sense that they are experiencing what the characters are experiencing. Chases and fights, for example, often use POV, handheld cameras in motion, fast pans, zooms—in fact, you'll need all the visual ammo you can muster.

What this requires is a multi-angle, multi-take approach to get all the shots to build a coherent scene. Plenty of Hollywood movies out there sacrifice coherence for their money shots: the explosions, stunts and effects. But if the coherence is lost in what you're trying to show – if your shots don't make sense when cut together – you lose tension and possibly your audience.

Be prepared. If you can't multi-take and you've just got one hit at that car-crash or decapitation, make sure you've got it covered. At the least, you need it to look good, but if it is that one pivotal scene that turns everything around in your movie, then you need it to be great.

Clockwise from above: Start off easy, then let the tension build steadily, until you reach the inevitable point of confrontation.

Below: Move fast and cut quick. While we could just take one long shot of the girl running, it works better to move in, using three shorter shots, to make the action feel more harried and kinetic.

Cut and Cover

Getting all the right shots that you need for any scene is the main reason why you chose to do a storyboard. An audience expects to be given enough information to understand a scene in a logical order. How you choose to shoot your shots (angles, lighting, focus) and cut them together (pregnant, kinetic) is a question of genre and your own creative style.

What you don't want to find in the edit is that you haven't got enough shots to cover your dialogue or explain what the scene is about.

To make sure that you do get all the right shots on the day, use your storyboard and shooting script. If you've had time to check out your location or set beforehand, you'll have an idea of each of the setups that you actually need to cover your scene. In film jargon, a setup is the placement of the camera for one take of all or part of a scene. It's up to you to decide how many different setups are required to make sure you've got enough angles and framings to edit your scene the way you want it. The more actors and action, or the more lengthy your scene, the more setups you'll need.

You might not be acting out the whole of the scene in a setup, though. To give an example, an average 100-minute contemporary summer blockbuster has about 1,600 setups in it. Most other movies have around half that to successfully tell their story. This puts the average use of a setup to around 7.5 seconds in all, which will be cut up into the entirety of the scene. Obviously, not many scenes are 7.5 seconds long, giving an idea as to how much is actually used of that particular setup in a Hollywood movie.

The way to work this on set is to ensure that you have your master shot. This is the most important shot that you'll have. The master shot is your entire scene played out in a framing that incorporates all the actors and the essential part of the set and the props.

The quickest way of shooting your scene is to shoot your master shot – plus a duplicate for safety – then shoot all the inserts that emphasize the points that you want to make. Your focus points will be close-ups of dialogue, props, points of view.

Within the close-ups of subjects, you'll need more than just tight shots of actors speaking. You also need appropriate reaction shots from the dialogue's recipient. As with the 'action' shots of the speaker, the reaction shots can be close-ups or shots taken over the shoulder of the speaker. When shooting either, it's important to place each subject correctly in frame.

If your speaker is on the left of frame for their close-up or over-the-shoulder shot, the reaction should place the subject on the right of frame. This is standard Hollywood language, and we all understand it.

However you shoot the scene, it's going to hit you hard in the edit that there are eyelines you don't like, expressions that don't work, camera wobbles, distracting passersby – and a host of other potential irritations. Because of this, you need to make sure that you've shot enough cutaways. Cutaways, or inserts, are shots that are meaningless in themselves, but make enough sense within the context of the scene that the audience won't really notice. The usual reason that you put such a shot in is that it can paper over all sorts of dodgy video and provide a seamless shot for the audio to continue over. Conversely, if you wish to chop your audio in the edit, they can allow this to happen without a jump-cut of the subject.

Examples of a cutaway might include a view out of a window, a hand picking up a cup of coffee, a close-up of your subject's eyes or shuffling feet. Shoot a long shot that you can cut to that doesn't betray obvious mouth movement. You're looking to find something that won't give you a continuity headache. Video is cheap and there are no excuses (unlike film) not to have enough footage.

Many Hollywood movies shoot dress rehearsals or use outtakes when then want a better reaction shot or a useful cutaway. Shoot tight on actors preparing to shoot or just

composing themselves. Slight obscurity or a random point-of-view shot can cover all evils, and help to pace or punctuate your edit.

This brings us onto the one thing to watch out for: shoot ratio. Your shooting ratio is the amount that you shoot versus the amount that you cut. In the classic Hollywood movie industry, the best directors knew what they wanted, shot it and used it, so getting a much lower shoot ratio. While this is neither here nor there with cheap videotape, it does make a difference in the edit. What you don't do is just run the camera and end up with a whole load of stuff to shuffle backwards and forwards through in the edit. It won't be great for your battery on the shoot either – let alone when you run out of tape completely and the nearest store is four hours' drive away.

Shoot reasonably sensibly, but above all make sure that you or the camera op is continuously logging shots. It's quite hard to be so disciplined on a hectic set, but once you've got into the swing of it you'll find it saves you time and money a month later when you've forgotten what you've shot in an edit.

There are various hi-tech methods of making sure you know exactly what's on each tape, but the best low-tech way is to get the camera op to shout out the time or timecode (if your camera gives you that information) for every shot or scene, and then write it down immediately. By the end of the day you'll have a list of numbers and descriptions that will be invaluable.

Top right: Shoot the master scene, shoot the dialogue action shots, then the reaction shots. It works for Hollywood, and it will work for you.

Above left, above, right: The storyboard, whether drawn or computerized, is your guide to getting the coverage you need. Previsualizing your scene is not just sensible, but essential.

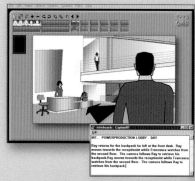

the final cut

Introduction

Editing is one of the most rewarding parts of filmmaking. You get to refine your story, controlling pace and style, all on your desktop. There is so much more to editing than simply choosing shots and sticking them together, although that is always your starting point.

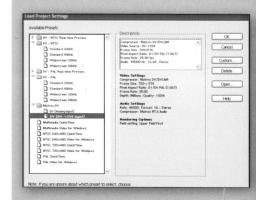

Your editing application and hardware will have most of your DV options built in. Choose the setting that matches what you shot, referring to the manual if you need to.

It pays to be organized, so it's essential that you have all the tools that you're going to need on hand. Your tools are your script, storyboards, shot-lists, tapes and a clear mind. The rest is equipment: a computer, editing software, a FireWire cable and your camera.

Be careful. Connecting FireWire can cause a sudden surge in power with 6-pin connectors, which can crash systems – especially if you're adding an external hard drive. Make sure your computer is switched on, your camera is switched on and only then make the connection from camera to computer.

When you create a new project in your editing software, you'll be asked to define settings for the whole project. First, set the video standard to either DV (NTSC) or DV (PAL), according to the camera you used. You then choose an aspect ratio, which is the shape of the screen. 4:3 is the square television screen, whereas 16:9 is widescreen,

and usually you should choose the aspect ratio you shot with. The exception comes if you want to put 4:3 footage into a 16:9 frame, which crops the top and bottom off to give you simulated widescreen.

For PC users with a specialist video card or FireWire card, you may need to choose a setting that lets the card and your edit software communicate. Check the relevant manuals for details. By finding the correct setting, you'll get the best performance out of your precious hardware. Lucky Mac users, can simply plug in the camera and go.

When you choose your settings, other decisions are automatically made for you. Frame size and frame

If you shot in 4:3, you can change your ratio to 16:9 at the edit stage. You'll lose the top and bottom of the frame and – if viewed on widescreen equipment – a small amount of vertical resolution.

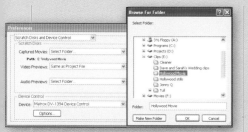

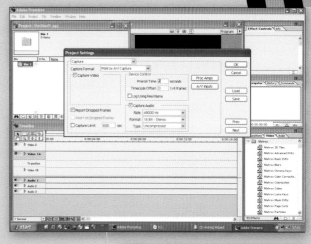

Moving the scratch disk to a separate hard drive is a sensible idea. It helps you to keep your material organized, and it means you're not putting too much of a burden on your system drive when it comes to processing the video data.

Right: Project settings in Adobe Premiere. Note tha *Preroll* and *Capture Audio* settings.

Below right: If you're working with NTSC DV, changing to *30 fps Drop-Frame* timecode will keep your project in sync throughout the edit. If you're using PAL, you don't need to worry.

rate will be set according to whether you're using North American NTSC or European PAL, but you don't really need to worry about them at this stage of the game.

To keep your project running smoothly through the editing process, you can also adjust the following preferences via the initial capture menu or the *Preferences* or *Options* menu (this will depend on your application). Getting these settings right at the outset can help you avoid problems later.

Scratch disk

This is the drive allocated to store your clips while you work on a project. The scratch disk is by default set to the same drive that your system runs from—your main hard drive. However, accessing clips on the same drive as the system software can slow things down, so change the scratch disk to another drive if you have one.

Audio settings

Audio files and clips are smaller than video clips and there's no reason to settle for anything less than 16-bit 48KHz audio. This will give you the CD-quality sound you need.

Device control

Your device is your camera, and *Device Control* lets you operate it via the desktop, enabling you to find clips and load them up through the application's interface, rather than fiddling with the camera controls. Set *Device Control* to a preset that recognizes your camera and any other video hardware.

Drop frame timecode

Because NTSC DV runs at 29.97 frames every second rather than 30 frames per second, the timecode of video doesn't relate to real time passing. A *Drop Frame* option means that the timecode is adjusted by one frame, every tenth minute to

compensate, so that an hour is counted as an hour. This just alters timecode – it doesn't take frames from the video itself – and if you're working with the European PAL DV standard, isn't even an issue.

Preroll and postroll

When you capture a clip, your camera needs a few seconds to get up to working speed. Set *Preroll* to about 3–5 seconds, and this gives your camera enough time to warm up – in fact, some cameras only need a couple of seconds. Set *Post-roll* to the same amount, and you'll give the camera time to slow down properly at the end of a clip without distorting the captured frames.

Finally, give yourself a second chance by using *Auto-Save*, as video files can crash some machines and you don't want to lose your work. However, auto-saving too much can make it tricky to unpick mistakes, so set it to run every ten minutes.

Importing the Footage

Your rough cut is the process of getting all your clips into the computer and assembling them in roughly the right order to tell your story – a moving storyboard, if you will. Your fine cut is where you finesse your clips, with all transitions, effects, graphics and titles in place. Start with the big issues, then work your way down to the details.

Begin by capturing clips from your video tapes. It sounds boring, but it's actually a vital part of the creative process, because you need to choose which takes to capture and which to discard. Don't attempt to capture every shoot from an entire reel. Although today's massive hard drives can handle the load, you should use your capture sessions to edit out the unwanted takes. At the same time, capture enough material to give you flexibility when editing. If there are three good takes of a particular shot, all containing good material, then capture them all so you can make creative choices later.

Capture

With your DV Cam connected to the computer via Firewire, and your software enabled, make sure that your camera is switched to video playback (VCR).

Professionals shuttle through video tapes using the J, K and L keys, which are standard shortcuts for Rewind, Stop and Play. Press L and your tape begins to play. The more times you press L, the faster the tape goes. You can slow it back

down with J. Press J often enough and the tape will play backwards. Using these keys you can rapidly navigate backwards and forwards through the tape. If you want to stop at any time, press K or the space

bar. It takes only a few moments to get used to these keys, and it's a far better way to work than using the mouse to click playback controls.

As you watch through your tape, mark the clips that you want to capture. You do this by setting *In*

and *Out* points, which are the places where you want the clip to begin and end. You mark an *In* point by pressing I, and an *Out* point by pressing O. These letters are placed just above the J, K and L keys, making navigation and marking clips a rapid process. Once you've marked *In* and *Out* points for a clip, click *Log*. The computer remembers your *In* and *Out* points for later, so that it can capture the clip when you've logged the whole tape. This means you can continue choosing and logging clips, concentrating on creative decisions, rather than waiting for the clip to load up into the computer.

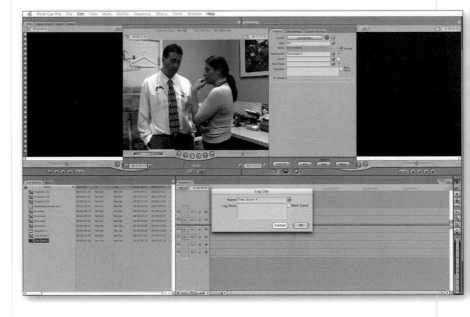

Batch capture lesson one. First, run through your footage and log the shots that you're going to use. Make sure you log everything you're going to need, but don't capture every take – the trimming process starts here.

Below: Logging in Adobe Premiere. Note the *In* points, the *Out* point, and a descriptive file name. If you really want to make things easier, add a comment in the *Log Comment* field. A few words now can save you time spent searching later.

Above left: Batch capture lesson two. Once you've logged all your clips, set your editing software to work. It runs through the tape and transfers the logged clips from the DV to hard disk.

Above right: Batch capture in operation. The editing software takes control of your DV camera, and grabs each clip according to your instructions.

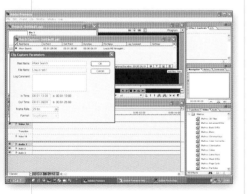

When you've run through an entire tape, marking all the *In* and *Out* points that you need, click *Batch Capture*. You can go and have lunch, while the computer searches through the tape for all your *In* and *Out* points, and automatically transfers your clips from your camera to your hard disk.

Rules

There are a few hard and fast rules to capturing that help things to run efficiently:

→ Capture to a different drive from your system drive, 3 to 5 seconds prior to your In point and after your Out point to allow for transitions.

→ If your software tells you a frame has been dropped, that means one or more frames weren't captured, and you should attempt capture again.

→ If you use a PC, don't try to capture clips longer than four minutes, as Windows may not let you, and clips of this size can cause crashes.

→ Label all of your captured clips with useful names that will help you to identify them. 'Coast (Anne2) 3' shows that it's the scene on the coast, that this was the second shot of Anne, and the third take. Purely descriptive names, such as 'Anne smiling', can make it difficult to locate the relevant shots.

Housekeeping

Keep tapes in date and roll order and in their boxes, and keep them rewound to protect them.

Good editing software, such as Final Cut Pro, lets you create folders called 'Bins' to store batches of clips. Each scene of your movie should be given its own bin, and all related clips should be stored there. This keeps everything organized, and saves lots of searching when you're editing scenes.

If you're using Final Cut Pro or something similar, your clips will have been captured at full resolution, and will play back at that resolution. In some inferior software, the resolution might appear to be worse. The data from the tape is still copied to your computer exactly, but the screen display will suffer. The final output will still be the same, so you'll just have to grin and bear it as you edit.

The Fourth Dimension

Place clips next to each other, and they begin to tell your story. Drag them to the *Timeline*, and you're starting to create your finished film. The timeline can be thought of as a desktop where you arrange your strips of video into a sequence. Every image, audio-clip, transition, effect, title and graphic can be manipulated in the *Timeline* to form a complete Hollywood movie.

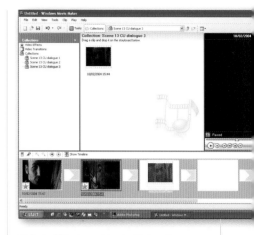

This is Windows Movie Maker in storyboard mode. Movie Maker makes it easy to drag and drop clips in place.

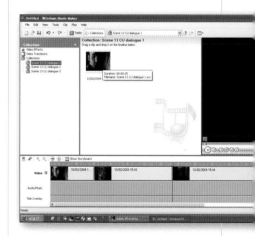

Switching to the *Timeline* mode brings up exactly what has been created as a storyboard, but then allows for all the tightening up that will create your Hollywood movie.

To add a captured clip to your movie, you drag it to the *Timeline*. When you press *Play*, you'll see the *Playhead* line move from left to right across the *Timeline*, as your clip plays in the window above. When you edit, you change the ordering of your clips on the *Timeline*, and adjust their length.

When starting out, work with one scene at a time rather than trying to complete the entire movie. You'll be surprised at how many shots you can discard, and eventually you will begin to remove entire scenes. The starting point, however, is to edit your scenes one at a time.

Storyboard mode

At first, your *Timeline* will probably appear quite simple, but its complexity will grow over time. Some beginners find it useful to create their first scenes with the storyboard mode, as it helps to keep everything simple. This is a first step – a rougher than rough-cut – to achieve your eventual *Timeline*.

Storyboard mode lets you put your clips in order, without editing them. When you're faced with a whole batch of different angles of the same scene, it can sometimes be really handy to see how the whole scene could work together. Storyboard mode can also show the strengths and weaknesses of your pacing, and whether or not you have got all the scenes and shots that you will actually need to tell your story.

The pro approach

Professionals tend to edit directly on the *Timeline*, rather than using storyboard mode, because it gives them far more control. Imagine that you need to use moments from three different takes of the same scene, dipping in and out of each clip as needed. Storyboard mode wouldn't allow you to do that, so when you need to get down to serious editing you'll need to see your work in the *Timeline*.

The simplest way to edit is to place clips one after another in Track 1 of the *Timeline* (*top right*). Where one clip ends and another begins, you have a cut. You can edit complete scenes in this way. You'll notice, however, that you can place

clips above track 1, in tracks 2, 3, 4 and so on (*above right*). You can stack clips on top of each other, and whichever is the highest clip is the one that will be visible in your movie. Imagine, for instance, that you want to cut between a master shot and two close-ups. There might

Above: Adobe Premiere's version of storyboarding has you assembling clips, then taking them to the *Timeline*. It's a more flexible way of working.

Above right and right: Pros prefer to work directly on the *Timeline*.

be fifteen cuts during the scene. Rather than dragging the clips to the *Timeline* fifteen times and shortening them, you simply drag all three clips onto their own layer. You then use the *Razor* tool to cut away the segments of the clips that you don't want to see. This approach is ideal for dialogue, when you're cutting back and forth rapidly between two shots.

One advantage of editing the digital way is that you don't need to worry about damaging clips when you cut them. The entire clip that you captured will remain untouched on your hard drive, no matter how many cuts you apply to it on the *Timeline*. This means that if you shortened a clip, you can easily lengthen it again, because the original data is still there.

Note that some low-end editing packages only have a single track for video and a single track for audio. Also be aware that some inferior applications won't let you add effects or transitions to anything other than Track 1. This won't stop you making your movie, but it will make the process more difficult.

88 Cutting the Movie

The best way to start editing any individual scene is to lay down your master shot. This will usually be the wide shot that shows the whole scene, revealing where you are and which characters are present. Some directors shoot the entire scene as a master shot, whereas others shoot only the opening, know that they'll cut to close-ups. If you've shot the entire scene as a master shot, then put the whole clip in the *Timeline*. Even if you don't use much of the master shot, it acts as a guide for placing other clips.

Most cuts within a scene are around three seconds long, and the general rule is that you start wide, go in to close-up, loosen up again and then go in tight for the denouement. That's standard language. If you understand that, then there's no reason at all why you can't play with undermining it. Remember, though, you're always trying to tell the story. Watch your favourite movies to see how these cuts are made, and begin to echo those patterns in your own work. When you drag the master shot to the *Timeline*, the master audio will also be placed in an audio track. This may not end up in the final mix, but it is a useful reference when cueing up other clips. When you're busy trimming clips over the master shot, remember to think about working the audio too.

While video simply cuts, audio jars unless there's extra audio baggage on either side of the clip to fade in and fade out. If you want to extend the audio to either side of a clip, first lock the video by clicking the padlock symbol. This lets you adjust the length of the audio without changing the video *In* and *Out* points. It's always useful to be able to extend a shot if you need to, but be aware that some software won't let you extend the clip if you *Razor* cut it. If that's the case, drag the *In* and *Out* point of the clip rather than chopping it. If you're using Final Cut Pro, you can *Razor* and drag at will.

There's a very fine line between maintaining tension (leaving a shot pregnant) and cutting to the chase. Sense the mood of your scene, the pace – and above all, choose your most emotional shot. Here's a classic quandary: is the cut from the master shot at the point of realization or the start of the action? A common rule is to cut on a movement or a look. If an actor looks up, moves a hand or turns away, that's a good time to cut, because the movement makes the cut feel less sudden.

It's easier to sync clips if you use strong visual references. Here, the *In* point is the rear emergence of the cop, and the *Out* point is the bag-grabbing. It is easy to sync these strong visual cues to the master clip.

You can, of course, cut the master track up as well, and you will probably need to do so. As you add more clips and trim them down, you will find that the scene probably runs more quickly than the master shot. If you're going to cut back to the master shot at any time, you will need to cut it up and shorten it for it to remain in sync with the other edits.

Create a new sequence for each scene, to avoid ending up with a timeline that runs for over an hour. This approach enables you to perfect each scene, and then drag all the sequences into one master sequence. You can then drag and drop entire scenes around this master timeline without having to select all the individual clips. It's then easy to move whole scenes, join them or drop them altogether.

Transitions

Digital video has something that many other forms of art don't: time. A painting is two-dimensional, a sculpture three-dimensional. Video, like music, has the fourth dimension of time. Whereas some art forms capture a moment, music and video reveal change over time. Editing gives you the opportunity to create the illusion of time passing, and to change the audience's emotional responses over an hour and a half.

It can be useful to think of movies as being like concertos or symphonies, changing moment to moment, but describing larger themes, with patterns of pace and momentum. Sometimes you want your audience to be aware of time ticking away, and sometimes you may want them to be so involved with the story that there is no sense of time passing. You need to show the audience the time that has passed between scenes, especially when those scenes are set in the same location. When you edit you are always dealing with time.

The cut

A hard cut involves no fading; one shot ends and the next begins. When watching dialogue scenes, we cut from one shot to the other every few seconds, and because we are listening to the characters talk, we don't notice the cut. You direct the audience's attention with each one.

Use a cut when you are working within the same scene to show that you're in the same space and time. Use a cut to cut against another scene in the same location, to create irony, parody, tension or conflict. Use a cut to create meaning through juxtaposition (show a man looking in a mirror and cut to a peacock).

The scene of the getaway here is followed by a scene at a dinner

party. The two scenes are very different and require the right transition between them. If you simply cut from one to the next, you may confuse or disorient the audience, as cuts always feel as though they occur within a scene. Instead, apply a dissolve, to fade one scene out while the other fades in.

There are audio issues to consider too, and often the best way of dealing with a transition is to work it with the audio. Here the audio transforms from incidental music to the sound of the music in the room, helping to indicate that we've cut from one time and place to another.

The dissolve

Applying transitions, such as dissolves and cross-fades, between clips is an essential part of explaining to an audience just how time is supposed to be passing. Mostly, you don't want your audience to realize that a cut has been made. When they watch a scene, they should notice everything that's going on except the edit points. When you move from one scene to another, however, you need your audience to know that time has passed and that we've moved somewhere new. Sometimes costuming, location and lighting are the only cues you need, but sometimes the sense of time passing is unclear, so you need to draw attention to the edit. This can be done by fading out, lowering the sound or using a dissolve.

Transitions are the equivalent of a comma in a sentence, offering a moment of pause before getting on with the next scene.

A dissolve transition carries the audience from one scene to another without the harsh edge of a hard cut. Transitions last from about half a second to two seconds, although even longer transitions can be used for a very gradual change.

For the audience, a dissolve lets a scene breathe into the next.

Use a cross-dissolve between two different scenes to imply the passing of time. Be aware that an audience will presume that only a small amount of time has passed, unless you give them specific dialogue or visual clues to determine the timing.

Use a cross-dissolve between lock-offs of the same scene to imply the passing of time. Infer or contradict the amount of time passed by manipulating an audience's perceptions of image change (beard growth; worn-out shoes; a burnt candle; an empty rail station).

Use a cross-dissolve between shots in the same scene only when confusing time through a character's perspective (dreams/drink/drugs). When a mix is taking an audience from one scene to another with either the same character or the same location, it's used as an explanation for the change in place

or subject. Adding a cross-dissolve as our character leaves a phone booth with the same character standing on a street tells a well-versed audience that a certain amount of time (indicated by captions or dialogue or not at all) has passed. If this was to work as a cut, the character would have to be shown leaving the phone booth before cutting to the character standing on the street.

The fade

When you want to imply that a huge amount of time has passed, or that one part of the film is completely over, you can fade out to black, then start the next scene.

As this gives the movie quite a long pause, most films contain only one or two fades at most. In other words, they shouldn't be used between every scene, but only when absolutely necessary.

The wipe

Wipes are transitions that reveal the second scene as the first is wiped away. The motion of the wipe is either vertical (bottom to top or vice versa), or horizontal (left to right, or vice versa). The edge of the wipe can also be graduated, softened or hard. The wipe isn't used very often in modern Hollywood, and when it is, it's used for a deliberately quirky or old-fashioned effect.

Here, we cut from a medium shot to a wide, and a passing car has been used to make the transition from one shot to another. This works because the last frame of the passing car is cut in exactly the same place as the first frame of the passing cop and a unity is formed.

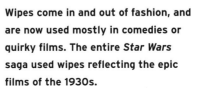

Wipes come in and out of fashion, and are now used mostly in comedies or quirky films. The entire *Star Wars* saga used wipes reflecting the epic films of the 1930s.

Movie Language and Timeline Tricks

When you get into the edit, you'll be surprised how your carefully contrived shots sometimes just don't work together, even when you managed to get all the shots you needed on the day. The good news is that your software is so versatile that, with a touch of creativity, there's always a way around these problems.

The issue is always how to translate the language of movies that you used on the shoot into the edit itself. Let's look at an example:

Here's the medium shot:

Here's the wide shot:

And here's the close-up:

The problem is that there is no shot that connects the actor standing, waiting for the phone to ring, with the actor answering the phone. She has to move into the call box, but there's no shot of her moving at all.

There are always solutions. This could be a job for a transition, but the scene is so firmly located and the phone call comes immediately after the passing of the constable, so a dissolve will confuse an audience as to how much time has passed.

A cutaway to another scene is always possible, so we can cut back to the actor in the call box, but this would then destroy any suspense created by the scene.

The alternative is to find a shot that can provide a link to join the other two shots together.

The answer comes in the form of an outtake of the actor putting the phone down and leaving the call box at the end of the shoot.

Leaving the call box? For the shot to make sense, she needs to enter an empty call box in order that the cut doesn't put her in two places (outside the call box/inside the call box) at once. How will the shot of her leaving help our cause?

Easy. Let's reverse the shot. Then, by applying new brightness (lowered) and contrast (raised) values to the clip, we turn it into a silhouette that doesn't give away any sign of being reversed. The clip can then be cut right up to the previous shot of the actor waiting.

This then leads perfectly logically to the next shot.

The one thing that remains? Provide an audio transition of the phone ringing. This seals the deal for the audience.

This example underlines why it is so important to shoot plenty of cut-aways on the day, so that you always have something to work with in an emergency.

Your task becomes more of a challenge when your shots contain dialogue that has to be delivered in a certain order. If lips are moving, the audience is particularly sensitive to any trickery. Dialogue scenes also require reference back to the 180-degree rule (*see page 74*). There are certain different angles that won't cut together without distracting an audience.

THE FINAL CUT

This scene has been shot loose with a free-roaming camera from the same side of the imaginary 180-degree line. That doesn't mean it's an easy job.

The camera has to cover a certain distance before it can avoid being a jump cut. While this cut works...

...this cut doesn't. Look for shots that refer to each other to ensure that you're cutting logically.

This shot cut against the next informs us that the first subject is looking at the second subject. The second shot informs us that the second subject is not looking back at the first subject.

In such cases only continuity-pleasing wides or mediums like this...

...or a reaction shot from the third subject like this will do. If the dialogue becomes a conflict or argument, the third subject can direct his attention straight to camera, so that we see him from the female's point of view. When an actor looks into camera the effect is quite unsettling for the audience, so you need to follow the shot with one that's equally strong. Perhaps the most logical choice is to cut to his POV to show her.

If you're bewildered by the choice of shots in front of you, refer back to your storyboard to remember what you were trying to achieve when you planned the scene originally.

Movie Magic

Most editing software comes complete with many visual effects filters, which are best used sparingly. It's not often that you would sit down in a cinema and watch these kinds of things in action.

It can be tempting, at first, to use every effect that's available to you, but as always, watch the feature films that you like and see how rarely such filters are used on shots. Although colour correction is used on many shots in a feature film, it's rare to find simple distortion filters being applied to a shot. Most filters actually degrade the image to some extent, so you must question whether the effect benefits the story.

There are some effects that can work well with your images. Sometimes you may be forced to use a silhouette, due to editing requirements, and the shot will need to be made more interesting.

Playing with digital effects can be fun, but do they really make a better movie? Remember the effects-crazy days of the 1980s pop video? Push your nostalgia aside, and think how you would react to them now.

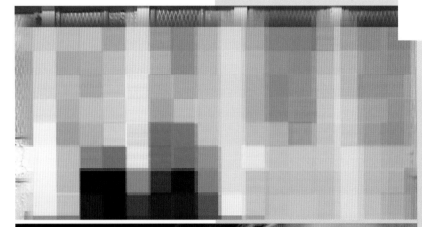

In the first example (*top*), the echo effect, coupled with a slowing of the clip's speed, will give the sequence a weird, dream-like quality. In the second example (*bottom*), filming the shot backwards then reversing it in software makes the killer's movements look strange and inhuman.

Here, a simple *Lens Flare* applied to the top of the subject's head gives the shot a little more visual interest. If not used deliberately, effects are just an amateur gimmick.

Using a blur or echo on your images with a slow motion rate (*right*) can enforce the sense of dreams, nightmares, flashbacks – anything seen from the perspective of the mind of the subject. This is standard Hollywood language, which means you're welcome to use it too, software permitting.

Sometimes, though, the magic is not a preset effect. This entire opening setup was created by shooting the action in reverse: the 'killer' started action over the shoulder of the subject and moved back into the shadows. By playing the clip in reverse (*right*), and cutting it up, a creepy effect is created; time appears to be moving forwards, but in a distorted way.

If you're still not happy with the fact that your digital video is pristine digital video and you want to give it a celluloid Hollywood movie effect, there are various ways to tackle the problem.

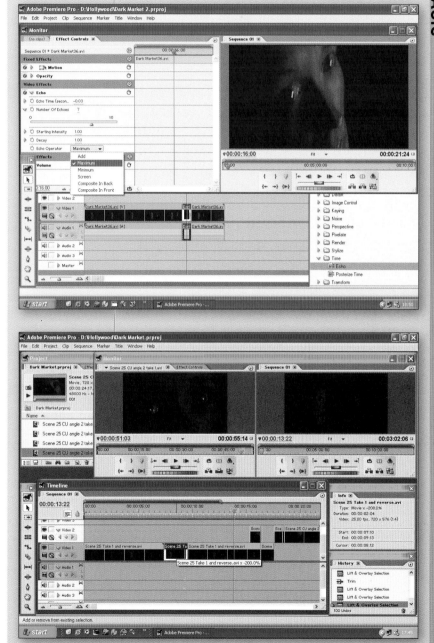

Many Film Effect filters are used to degrade the image, to resemble old film. Your picture will end up dirty, scratchy and noisy – and transformed to either black and white or sepia.

Here are the filters offered in Windows Movie Maker. While some are interesting, they're aimed more at the excitable amateur than the budding movie mogul.

The selection you get with a Matrox XtremePro card running through Premiere Pro covers more ground, and the effects are of more use to the professional.

Some 'old film' effects can be surprisingly successful, but the fact is that your video is video, shot at either 50 or 60 fields every second and not with the 24 frames that film has at normal running speed. If you want to get that slightly animated, motion-blur effect of film, then you should also use a *De-Interlace* filter on your footage.

Filters and effects work best in combination. Use colour correction to desaturate an image, then add a *Glow* filter or a *Lens Flare*. Don't be half-hearted if you're going to leave the real world behind.

You can also use some filters to limit the effect of others, so that a glow is applied to only part of the image. If you apply a 4-point garbage matte to an image, this lets you draw a line around the part of the clip that you want to change. So you could draw a line around the clock on the wall, then apply a *Glow* filter. That means that only the clock will glow. This subtle approach is much more effective than just applying filters to entire clips.

Left from top:
This Quicktime Effects *Faded Color Film* plug-in allows for the amount of noise and scratch to be input on sliding scales.

Here, the two scenes have been slightly degenerated using a *Monochrome Noise* filter. The colour has already been desaturated, so some colour correction could be used to bump the tones up a bit.

In this example, colour correction has been used to desaturate the image, and a *Glow* filter has been applied to make the water on the window sparkle.

102 Colour Correction

The production values of your Hollywood movie will be affected by the overall look you choose for the piece. Rich, saturated colours always smack of opulence, just as contrasting black and white speaks of classiness. If you want to emulate the feel of film noir, you'll be looking for a monochrome picture, and if you want to shoot day for night, the language of the movie calls for a more bluish tinge to your scene.

High-end software, such as Final Cut Pro, gives you control over the colour of shadows, midtones and highlights. You can, for example, make the glow on somebody's face just a little bit more yellow, without changing the blue sky behind them. On a fast system colour correction works in real time, so you can make adjustments to your clip and watch them instantly, without having to wait for a lengthy render.

Although the filter you'll use is usually called colour correction, industry professionals refer to the process as 'colour grading'. When a motion picture is assembled, every shot is colour graded to create a particular look and feel for each scene. Sometimes, this colour grading allows dim, bluish shots that were taken late in the day to match the colour of afternoon shots. Or you might colour an entire scene to create a particular atmosphere. Colour is also used symbolically, so you could use gold light to represent wealth, or blue light to represent a cold, broken relationship.

This particular shoot was undertaken on a gloomy day. If it looked stylish with a sense of oppression, it might work: instead, it just looks drab. In fact, the whole scene – aside from a setup where the clouds parted a little – is looking grim. The idea is that the scene will be quite stark in its look, with contrast and heavy blacks creating a gritty, dirty feel.

The gloom is a product of the lack of light. Therefore, it's the brightness that needs to be changed (right) for the whole of the scene bar the shots that had the benefit of sun. Scenes like this should only be exported for doctoring if they are a series of cuts with no transitions. Shots that don't need the same values applied can be dealt with separately. Simply scanning through each setup will allow you to work out how far you go before you need to change a setting.

Your software will either require you to click on a clip or drag an effect to change the *Brightness* and *Contrast*, then a control window will let you tweak. In this case, a white window is in danger of becoming indefinite against the dark bricks. It's a balance between getting the desired contrast and not overilluminating the scene.

Now that these *Brightness* and *Contrast* values are right for the first clip up to the razored change in light,

it's quicker to stick with the same clip and apply the changes in colour. Colour correctors differ in the way that they are applied to the clip, and the interface that they use. What they share in common is that they have presets which you might find useful, and that they offer infinite values for how your image can look. Using the sliders, here, a noir-ish blue has cooled the image down.

By lowering both the *Saturation* of colour and deepening the *Black Output* level, the requisite look will be created.

Vectorscopes are extremely popular devices for controlling the colour in an image, particularly for broadcast-quality programmes. This is the visualization of the colour correction just applied, and shows that any saturation present in the image leans towards Blue/Cyan and Red - this is just where you want it.

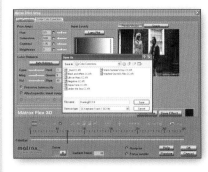

If you're lucky, you can save off the new *Hue* and *Saturation* effect that you've created; it'll help you a lot. If not, write down your settings because you will need them again.

The reason? You'll need to apply the colour correction values to every razored clip. In Final Cut Pro you can drag colour correction settings to a whole batch of clips in one go.

With grading like this, the amount of time and patience you will need to maintain consistent grading pays off when you export your final footage. Your production values are already looking more expensive!

Don't spend too much time perfecting the first clip that you work on, because as you adjust other clips in the scene, you may want to come back and make changes to the first clip. Colour grading is time-consuming, and requires skill. Avoid the temptation to make everything as bright and colourful as possible. Your priority should be to ensure that each scene has perfectly matched shots, and that your colour balance reflects the style of your movie.

If you're aiming for broadcast or just a TV-friendly DVD, there are limits to how saturated and how bright your colours can be. Apply a *Broadcast Legal* filter when everything else has been done.

Working with Titles

A movie without a title is a dog without a name. If it doesn't have one, you can't call it anything, you can't write it on the DVD cover, you can't chalk it up on your CV. Any writer with any pride will have named their movie, no matter if it gets changed along the way.

Adding titles makes your movie worthy of an audience. Titles come in three different types: opening titles, in-movie titles and closing titles. Your titles should be clear enough and on screen long enough to be read easily.

There are three fundamental ways that titles can work. They can appear as stills, rolls (vertical) or crawls (horizontal). Most modern software allows for stills, rolls and crawls to be created with a click, as well as a plethora of other fancy moves and transitions as presets.

Opening titles

Opening titles incorporate the name of the movie. The exceptions that prove the rule, though, are becoming more and more common. Often, these days, the way of involving an audience from the start is to go headlong into the movie without a title or opening titles. Standard practice, though, is to credit the producer, director and main actors, then state the title, then credit supporting actors, the main crew and the writers, producers, and director (again). Don't be embarrassed to put your name up front if you're the director, because

if you get your film into a festival, or broadcast on television, you want to be recognized for your hard work.

Find a way of presenting the title that works with your movie.

Recall the theme of the movie again and think about using this for the title. If it's about death, might the title float up and disappear? If it's about cloning, might the title divide into two? If the title's on your first scene, work it in with the image or the feel of

the scene. If it's during the autumn, would the title drift down the screen? If two people bump into each other in the street, would the title crawl in from either side and meet in centre frame? If your title is placed over the opening scene of the video, make sure that there's nothing going on behind it that will make it difficult to read.

However you do it, ensure that the title is on screen for about three seconds in its nontransitional state. Any more and it's laboured; any less and it's illegible.

Final Cut Pro's LiveType is a fantastically comprehensive title generator, with animated fonts and backgrounds, giving you broadcast-quality titles in just a few clicks.

G-Gnome created by A. Sarah Mayfield

Make-Up Simon Dupont
Prosthetics Kathryn Fleet
Stills Jennie Jones
Lou__ __larkson

Runner Gina Martin
Artwork Dave Downes
Belinda created by Eric Moore
Graphic Design Michelle Horton

Kit Hire Metro Video
Post Production Oasis Television
Editor Amrit Bharry
Audio Mixer Pete Collins
Telecine Rushes

Closing titles

Closing titles acknowledge the people who have helped make it all possible. And why should an audience care? Well, they don't usually, which is why it's your job to make them as entertaining as possible. A final tie-up scene for an incidental character, sing-along music, outtakes – even specially shot out-takes – all make an audience (and not just the crew) sit in their seats until the movie plays out.

Closing titles roll from the bottom of frame to the top (only a few dare do it from top to bottom). Hollywood movies use this method as they have a lot of people to credit. You may not, which allows for a certain freedom from this easily-typed tradition. Do try and remember everybody. If somebody gets left out, you've lost one helpful soul the next time round (although your mum will probably still make the cup of tea that helped you through the long edit).

If you don't use opening titles, be sure to credit your key cast and crew at the end, in the same order you'd have used at the beginning, except for the director, who should (of course) appear first.

If you've finished your movie with a punch, it's essential that your titles don't change the mood unexpectedly. In this case we're led to believe that - strangely enough - the killer isn't dead at all. There were no titles at the beginning of the film, which means the name of the movie indicates the end of the film. Going out with a *Digital Zoom* allows the title to come in with a *Cross Zoom* for maximum effect. Mixing to a *White Matte* lets the shadow appear on the font and adding a *Lens Flare* to its roll motion creates the transition out of frame.

In-movie titles

In-movie titles include subtitles, captions, chapter headings, character translations or text to create quirky moments. Unless you're remaking *Dances with Wolves*, you shouldn't need to use this sort of title much, but if you do then it needs to be legible. Don't worry if your titles look dull – it probably means your audience can read them. When it comes to time on screen, you may find it's dictated by the amount of time that someone spends saying or doing something, but try to give them enough time to be read.

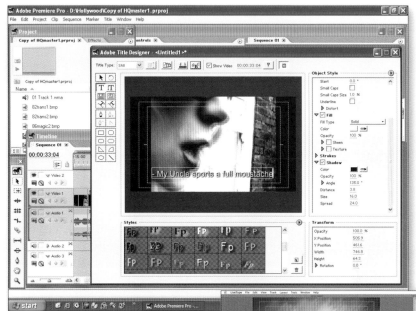

Working against a moving background, make sure that your quirk or your joke doesn't collide with any of the images by using sans serif, bold, filled fonts with shadow.

Titles say that the movie is finished, that it has a beginning and it has an end. There's still some way to go, however, before you see the end of your movie.

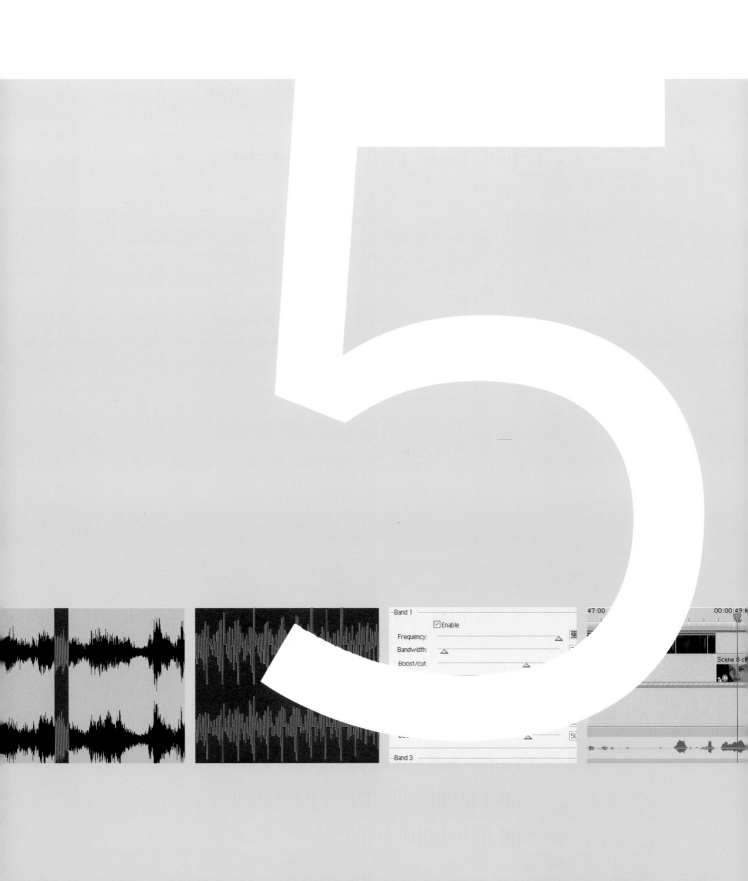

editing audio

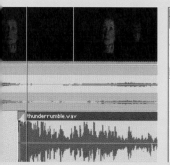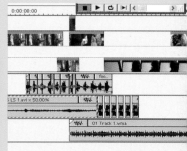

Introduction

Audio is given a rough ride. It's there, always attached to your clip, doing its thing adequately with no frills, letting the visuals take centre stage. How dull. It's time to turn things around and put audio centre stage.

Below: By studying the waveforms you can visualize your audio, enabling you to work with the dynamics and make the soundtrack work with the clips on the *Timeline*.

All audio has a dynamic range. That is to say that it has a variable range of output values – decibels (Db) – from high (loud) to low (quiet). An orchestral work that varies in range (Haydn's *Surprise Symphony*, for example) has a wide dynamic range; a thrash metal track that is just loud has a narrow dynamic range. For loud tracks, digital audio is very different from a standard hi-fi system. It's so sensitive to noise that anything set over 0Db will be interpreted as distorted. Always keep this in mind when working with audio in your edit.

Audio can be visual too, and most editing packages have the ability to expand the audio tracks into a comprehensive waveform. Simply by looking at your *Timeline* you'll be able to see your entire dynamic range, running from narrow (quiet) to wide (loud).

Editing audio is exactly like editing pictures in theory – chunks of clips that can be cut, copied, pasted and razored as you will. However, your interface will treat them slightly differently. The first difference is the fact that while on a multiple track edit, only the top layer of video will be visible, every layer of audio will play through when you press play.

Below: Audio can be edited just like video, but you need to be aware that every layer will be audible, not just the top one. As a result, your soundtrack requires careful mixing.

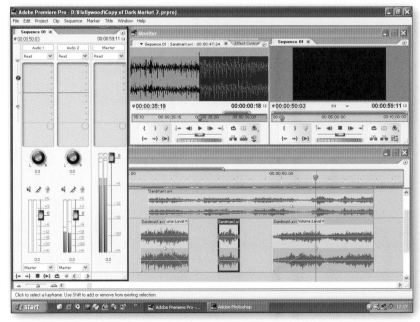

While cuts in video can be made easy on the eye through continuity, to make audio easy on the ear requires audio mixing. Indeed, the second crucial way that audio differs from video is actually the way that the viewer processes the information – just as the relatively small data of audio is rendered much quicker than video by the computer, so we are much quicker to notice differences in it. For this reason, it's very hard to simply cut audio. It has to be mixed in and mixed out to some degree. This is a similar practice to the way we use cross-dissolves in video.

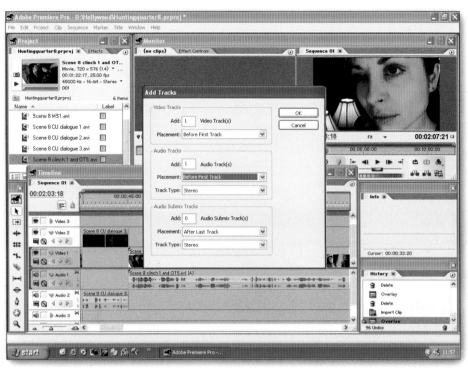

Even a change in scene doesn't qualify for just an audio cut. If you look and listen to any Hollywood movie, the sound doesn't just cut into a scene. It flows from one to another. If the point is to create a contrast – somebody sits home alone in a quiet house cut against a club scene – the club music will be contrived to cut on the beat, making the change in audio less harsh on the audience. However disturbing the movie, it's not supposed to be a sensually unpleasant experience.

Sync audio will by default be linked to the video, and video placed on certain tracks may well cover existing audio that you'll always find you want. If in doubt, add audio and video tracks separately to make sure that you've got everything at your fingertips.

To make sure that you're not covering important tracks in a multiple audio track interface, be regimented about your audio clips. Imagine what you are going to need and create the necessary audio tracks from the start.

There are four different types of audio: dialogue, sound effects, music and Voice Of God (or voice-over). Dedicate at least one track to any of these that you are going to use, bearing in mind that there are going to be times when you have to mix one sound effect with another (i.e. you'll need two tracks set aside for sound effects).

Last, and certainly not least, remember that there are as many different file formats for audio as there are for video. Some files are entirely incompatible with your

To deal with the complexities of synchronized audio and video, add extra tracks to give yourself enough room to maneuver.

Timeline. Most editing packages won't take .MID or .CDA files – the type most consumer CDs are written to. They contain lots of other data that is not recognized. MP3 files, meanwhile, are so compressed that it takes a really good audio codec to get usable audio out of it. Try and stick with the .WAV (PC) and .AIFF (Mac) formats, as these will be digestible for most computers and most applications.

Controlling Volume

The essential part of any audio experience is the volume. It sounds quite elementary - and it should be. Like pacing your video edit, volume should be there to keep your audience hanging onto every word: they can't do this if it's too quiet, and they won't do this if it's too loud.

When you're in your audio edit, make sure that the volume settings on your computer and on your speaker system are set at medium. Check this every time you get into the edit to make sure that when you export, your levels aren't all over the place. Always have your audio tracks expanded if you can to give an idea of their dynamic range.

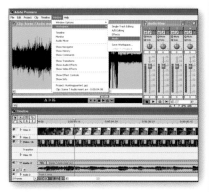

The three tracks here in descending order are atmos, sync dialogue and music. While the atmos and music continue throughout the scene, the dialogue is the one bit of audio that is just stuck there. That's the bit that is obviously going to hurt unless something is done.

Because audio is so sensitive, you need to try and find a way with your edit software to get the most detail out of your audio clip. Some apps have specific workspaces for audio, which make the whole process a lot less painful.

With any audio inserts like this, it's the integration into the rest of the sound that is important. In this situation where the atmos and music continue throughout, it's a question of volume, and the way to achieve the integration is by fading into your audio insert and then out again. To do this, make sure that you have enough lead in and out of your insert to make the fade in and out as gradual as possible. About two seconds on either side is the kind of length that makes it easier to play with, but you may not need that much if there's little difference in volume between the insert clip and the rest of your audio.

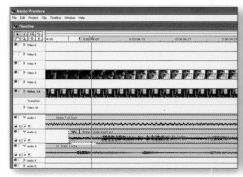

The change from background noise to dialogue on the clip can clearly be seen with the audio as a waveform. A lot of software uses volume control as a 'rubber band' on tracks. The objective is to create an incline from the start of the clip (background noise) to the start of the dialogue. Clicking on the rubber band creates keyframes for your audio that can then be dragged to the volume control of choice – the bottom of the track being mute, the top being maximum decibel.

Doing exactly the same thing in reverse (a decline) at the end of the audio insert will give you the seamless entry and exit that your clip requires.

Sometimes, your audio edit is not a simple question of sounding nice through sync and mix. This audio insert has the added responsibility in making the audience believe that there is a brief time compression between the end of this clip with the actor waiting...

isn't even a Guinness World Record. Slow-motion could be applied to these eight frames, but it would be noticeable with the hand-held camera. Besides, there is no need, as we can use audio to command the situation.

The language of cinema dictates that a sudden change in audio also means a change of time and place. That doesn't mean the location itself needs to change, just the position or angle of the camera. On the *Timeline*, putting the recorded phone-ring effect onto an audio track will compress time for the audience and still maintain believability.

A change in audio can also be a change in volume. It means that the audience, identifying with the

One of the most important points at which to raise volume is any situation where you might have a surprise or 'jump shot'. These tend to find their way into horror movies, and are the springboard (rather than the ramp) to action sequences. In order to create the effect, everything up to that point in the sequence has to be dropped in audio – remember, even the accompanying 'jump' audio cannot be levelled over 0Db. The audio for this horror moment needed just that bit extra for the first flicker of illumination of the killer appearing in the background. Given that there's a certain irony in the overused shot, a downloaded thunder effect is the perfect way to puncture the existing soundtrack. Thundercracks are great for these moments as they naturally start at a harsh 0Db and work down. Because it is a downloaded 8-bit effect, a small cross-fade covers any significant change in audio quality that might disturb the audience.

...and the beginning of the next frame with the actor entering the call box. There are eight frames of the booth without the actor in it. One-third of a second from a waiting position to appearing in a call box

subject, is closer to the source of the audio. It might seem like a huge responsibility for the audio to make this change in environment believable, but it can do so just by raising the volume at a cut.

Talking Pictures

The audio in a dialogue scene needs to flow. If you've shot a few takes on the same day in a closed frame, the one thing that you should have on your side is that there are no discrepancies in the levels of audio and the type of sound that you have.

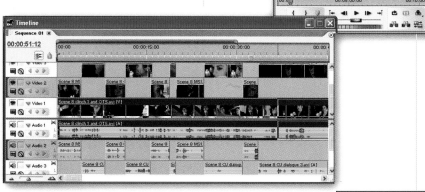

Because audio is less fussy than video when it comes to rendering, it's easier to deal with when there's more on the *Timeline* than less. Because of this, razoring isn't going to help you with creating seamless dialogue because it won't let you paper over the cuts.

Papering cuts and making an audience believe in the *Timeline* of the movie is down to transitions and cutaways with video; with sound, it's the entire audio capture. Sometimes, making is unbreaking.

In the example above, the multiple track *Timeline* has been constructed as a chequerboard. This means that there is space to mix dialogue

through from each clip to another. What you don't want is for the video clips to mix through as well. By default, the audio and video clips will be linked to each other, and will need unlinking so that you can get the dialogue that you want.

Unless you've a very long dialogue scene, loose shooting or shooting on the fly is best captured as an entire take. The reason for this concerns the audio, which is the most important part of any dialogue scene. This sequence just has four takes, each of which can be dragged to the *Timeline* time and time again, and each clip on the *Timeline* has *In* and *Out* points dragged. Loosely-shot dialogue scenes require maximum flexibility on the *Timeline* because your audio needs to be as versatile as possible to cover the cracks in your footage.

Unlinking the audio and having it draggable at both the *In* and *Out* points allows the audio clips to be extended into the previous clip for a few frames. What this does is continue any noticeable atmos, audio pregnancy, actor breaths – anything that isn't part of the dialogue itself. Drag out the end or the beginning of whichever track is more efficient or more pertinent.

Double tracks, though, mean double volume – and this in itself is a useful tip should you wish to increase a clip's volume without tipping it over 0Db (just duplicate it in exactly the same place on a different track). So, for those few frames of audio overlap, the volume will be noticeably louder.

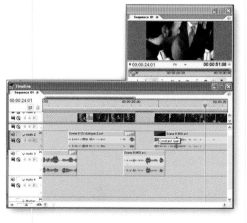

Just as you might have performed a cross-fade between two clips, you need to mix one track up and the other down over the duration of these frames to counteract their volume. This can either be done with your rubber bands, by decreasing the volume on the out audio and increasing it on the in audio, or (in some applications) by using an audio cross-fade.

This process is repeated all the way down the *Timeline* until all the audio blends unnoticeably together.

Of course, all of this relies on your video clips displaying sync all the time. While this is the only way of working audio with some single-track editing packages, sometimes it can just get a little...dull. If you look at a Hollywood movie, you'll find that a hefty proportion of lines don't ever manage to get to the end of the shot before the visual cuts away. Usually, this is a reaction shot where you wish for your dialogue to continue from one person off screen to the visual reaction on screen. This is, again, why multiple tracks with unrazored clips make the edit a happier place for your dialogue. Extending the dialogue audio underneath the reaction shot and cross-fading at the outro creates a slightly more sophisticated feel to the audio.

If you've put your audio and video together for a dialogue sequence, what can often happen is that the shot that accompanies one line of dialogue doesn't work – or the right shot has a faulty bit of audio. It's all fixable.

There are a few ways of dealing with this headache. ADR – additional dialogue recording – relies on the actor to come into the edit and sync the line with a hot-plugged mic. It'll take a few tries, but it'll happen.

Another way is to use a cutaway over the actor and cut back to one where the shot is good enough. You don't have to do either of these, though. If you've got a problem, the first thing is to get somebody else in. Let them listen to the dialogue and see if the scene makes sense without the problem line in place. You may be precious about your script, but sometimes there are things that are better left unsaid.

Audio Filters

Because dialogue is the one main audio source for progressing the story, it's important that it isn't distracting or subject to hum or hiss. This is all to do with how you miked your shoot, what audio sources you've recorded and what frequencies they play within and over.

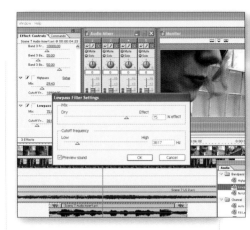

The differences on location can be very slight, and in the edit very noticeable. Miking from above will always record the higher frequencies of the voice better. From below, it's exactly the opposite, as deeper reverberations from an actor's chest weight the sound.

First things first. Locations are terrible for background noise, and even wearing closed headphones doesn't help after a period of time: you eventually get a deaf spot for erroneous atmos. In the edit, this is where EQs (equalizers) come into their own. An EQ is a device that cuts off or boosts certain frequencies in your audio signal. If you don't have an EQ in your edit program, think about downloading or buying a separate one – and preferably one that will plug-in to your edit software, so that you don't have to switch programs to use it.

Once you've got the audio in the right place and the run in and out right, a 'first fix' audio-mix should be your next stop.

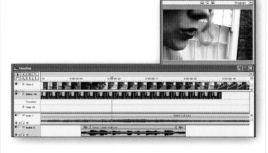

There's too much background noise on this clip and it's a very different background sound from the atmos track, as the insert was shot later in the day. It's also during the quiet intro of the music, which makes the dialogue just too loud.

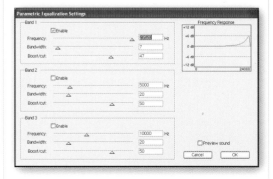

Listening to your audio through preview mode, it might become apparent that there is hiss or hum from background noise or interference. Filter this out with bandpasses. These tell the computer that you don't wish to hear certain general frequencies, as specified by a filtration value. Bandpasses can either be a highpass (high frequencies), or a lowpass (low frequencies), and they help to add clarity to your isolated audio.

Using an EQ on the audio insert also helps lift the dialogue out from the background noise. The dialogue is coming through at a higher frequency than the background street noise. By isolating it to a small bandwidth, the spoken lines are made more pronounced and the background noise is softened a little.

The lower frequencies in audio are accompanied by hum, and the higher frequencies by hiss. The ear finds the hiss the more distracting, and an EQ will help take this away. If the background noise displays too much hiss or hum, a high or low bandpass can be used to remove the sound you don't want.

You won't have to do this for every clip. Most setups in a scene will have the same kind of sound throughout: dry in a furnished room or hollow in an unfurnished one, or popping if the mic was too close. Don't worry. When your audio's on the *Timeline* with your clips, any EQ-ing can be applied to one clip then copied and pasted to another.

Wearing headphones will help you to monitor audio on location, but there comes a point where you lose your sensitivity to the background racket.

If you've been directing, operating the camera and listening out for the audio, it's likely that your main concerns were the actors, followed by the shot, leaving audio on the backseat somewhere. If this sounds familiar, it would be smart to invest in some effective audio filters for your editing software.

All audio signals travel with a sine wave of frequencies. By default, your software will play out all sound as a 'flat' frequency, containing an average of all frequencies that form your audio. In effect, it's working like the ear without the brain. The brain picks up the frequencies we want to hear and discards those we

don't. That's why audio ops get a deaf spot for background noise – they're only human. Audio effects and mixers take over from the brain to do the same job.

Holding the mic high gives your dialogue a clearer, sweeter sound. Keep it down low, and reverb from the actors' chests adds a touch of muddy bass to the mix.

Original Soundtracks

Music is a thoroughly overwrought issue in the Hollywood movie. To be cynical, there are enough large studios that own enough record labels to double-whammy sales of both. Music is also thoroughly overused in the Hollywood movie, partly because of this and partly because it is now generally perceived as part of the movie entertainment experience. Got a romantic moment? Put in a ballad. Want to adrenalize your action sequence? Put in some hardcore drum and bass.

This sequence has a video transition to take us from the action getaway to a quiet cocktail party. The music has built in the action sequence, resulting in a hideous clash between the two different scenes. One way to tackle this is to turn it around and play on the irony of the two scenes together.

There are two different types of movie music: incidental and practical. Incidental music comprises the themes and background music of your movie, to reflect, accentuate, downplay or dramatize the feelings that you're creating in your scenes.

Practical music covers any music that can be explained in the natural world of the shot – music in clubs, music on the radio, music from the television and so on. The problem with practical music is that it has to sound half decent to be believable, which raises copyright issues if you're aiming for broadcast or theatrical distribution. Any third-party distributor will want to keep everything legit, and even Web distribution is a contentious form with regards to rights.

If you 'publish and be damned', all you rely on is somebody not hearing what you've done. It's unlikely that you'll be dragged through the courts – rather you'll be asked to remove the track – but the possibility is there.

Having said that, there are plenty of other ways to get hold of half-decent music – one of which is to use copyright-free music CDs, which tend to be just that: half decent.

If you are taking music into your movie from CDs, keep an eye out for various file formats that may not be read by your edit software. Audio CDs use .CDA files, which need to be ripped and usually re-encoded as an .AIFF or .WAV file before they will sit nicely on your *Timeline*.

For incidental music, there are rights-free CDs or cheap downloads available. What you might try and do if you have the energy is to create your own themes. Simple sequencers make it easy to import sounds, tracks or audio. Slowing them down, speeding them up, layering them, adding a beat – it's not rocket science and, while you probably won't get a hit spin-off record, you will have something unique. Of course, working with practical and incidental music brings some more creative problems.

Importing the same music and placing it on a new audio track allows the music to continue throughout the cocktail party.

different speeds (slow motion; slow motion; fast motion) and effects (echo; jitter; zoom/blur). The outcome of this is that the existing audio track (background noise of a radio station) is slow and strange.

As said, doubling up the same audio track doubles up the sound. Because the music kicks in as the subject begins to run away, dragging the second music track to this point gives the soundtrack extra drama at that point. This is a good thing, because the music becomes noticeably thinner at the point of the transition between clips. To make the difference in audio between the scenes even more noticeable, a decreasing pitch shift applied to the audio during the transition turns the pumping music to the duller sound you would find inside a dead room.

All the music transition now needs is a transitional decrease in volume for the first track and a lowered gain value for the second, so that the original eases into the same low throb that the closed frame and the furnished room need to sound like practical background music.

Using this kind of audio to an advantage is one of your best weapons. Sometimes audio like this can never be recreated. It's actually the second speed of audio at 30 per cent that sounds the most disturbing – giving us the required effect. Because your audio is multi-layered, it's easy to get a horrific sound. Slowing tracks, copying, razoring, pasting and reversing their speed as a separate layer is a great way of achieving this. Listen for sounds that accompany your effects. Isolating and razoring out certain bits of audio to marry with the jitters and the final zoom can add an incidental touch to a practical soundtrack. Don't be afraid of the process.

Applying the same pitch shift to the music track that takes over gives it that same muted effect.

Alternatively, you can create your own soundtrack. The end of this horror movie shows the killer alive and well and ready to take on the audience. It's a one-shot scene that is razored into three to apply

Dubbing Audio

Getting into an edit and being disappointed with the sound that you've recorded is not uncommon. While closed headphones out on location are your best weapon, it takes a good audio op to have less of a deaf spot than anyone else. There are ways of fixing things, though, given the right audio tools at your fingertips, and many of these can be found in your editing software.

Moving the copied clips apart on the *Timeline*, with enough believable pauses between each ring, takes the character from waiting to entering the call box without question.

The audio for this shot was made via a mobile phone outside the call box, allowing an external mic to pick up both the ring and the sound of the lift from the cradle. Sadly, the mobile phone has left an irritating buzz on the soundtrack.

Using a *Noise Gate* and dragging the sliders, specific frequencies can be eliminated from the sound. A noise gate with a high *Threshold* cuts out the sound and leaves the good ring as clear as a bell.

The final touch is simply to drag the lift from the cradle out from the end of the last audio clip to sync with the actor lifting the phone.

This shows how much weight audio holds. While you might think that video creates all the necessary transitions, it's actually the audio that joins the scene together.

Foley and dubbing are just as important. And if you haven't got the perfect sound from location or on set, there are other ways to find what you need. There are plenty of royalty-free sound-effect CDs out there, from horror to cartoon, and you can even find some vaguely usable music if you're lucky.

When played on the *Timeline*, the audio clip has one ring that has less buzz than the others. This gives us something to work with.

One ring, though, isn't good enough. Copying and pasting the ring next to each other is close, but makes the phone sound too urgent.

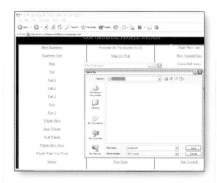

The alternative is to download sounds from the Internet. It might take a bit of searching to find the right sample, but remember that there are many ways of changing an average sound into a close-to-perfect sound, if your software has the capability.

The idea of using this footsteps-on-gravel sound effect is to provide a beat to lead into the intro of the music—a cop on the beat, if you will. The original audio has bits and pieces of traffic that don't provide the clear entry we're looking for. We don't want gritty hyper-reality, we want slick Hollywood sound.

We put the footsteps on the *Timeline* at the point at which the bobby is about to enter frame. Sadly, playing it back shows that it's too fast for the actor's measured pace. There appears to be one and a half footsteps for each of the bobby's, so slowing it down to 66% should be about right.

It's close, but it's not long enough for the clip. The point of suspense is the timing – here, the time spent waiting. To make that nervous wait longer, the footsteps should approach well before the bobby hits the picture and after into the phone-ring effect, to increase the feeling of danger. Copying the clip and pasting the duplicate next door adds to the duration and helps the soundtrack lead into the telephone-ring audio. Increasing and decreasing the volume will provide the subject's audio perspective – the footsteps approach, recede and, after a moment, disappear.

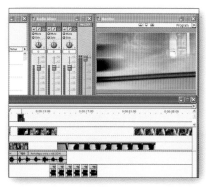

Finally, the footsteps have to form the start of the beat to the music intro. Moving the music up to the middle of the footstep audio is the first step. There are two ways of introducing the music: either to increase the volume from 0Db and

increase it as the footsteps die out, or to simply cut the natural start of the music in. Choosing the latter, it's always important that the music – as an intrusion into the movie from logical sync – cuts in at the right place. The right place tends to be when something is happening on screen, whether a cut, the start of action, a movement or another audio sting. In this case, it makes sense that it is the passing of the car that wipes to the wide.

The problem with the intro to the music is that it's supposed to carry through to the next scene. It doesn't. The heavy beat kicks in quite apparently on the waveform as the subject is still in the call box.

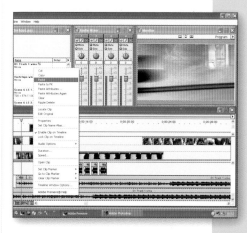

Creating another audio track and copying the same music track onto it loops any sound.

Waveforms make it easy with music because beats don't usually change within a track. Matching the beat with one track above the other is just a drag away, as is decreasing the volume of the first music track to let the second mix through and carry on playing the intro. Job done.

Mixing and Panning

Audio, just like images, can be fiddled with until the cows come home. What you really want, though, is to be able to shut the noise gate before the cows bolt again. The first step is to consider the audio before you export the movie. Look at your movie; listen to your sound; do them together and do them separately. If there's anything that itches, scratch it now before you tear your hair out.

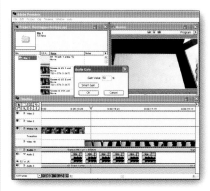

The rings for this telephone are too loud into the soundtrack. The audience is also going from two locations: one is a medium shot, the other a close-up inside the call box. Ideally, their whole tone would be softer and change from one shot to another. Using lower percentages of *Gain* allow this to happen.

With a half *Gain* value, the sync of the phone being lifted from the cradle is now lost – and it's an effect worth keeping. Increasing the volume level after the last ring and before the effect, by using rubber bands, brings the sound effect out from the background.

Within the same scene, the cop walks from right to left. To make use of stereo, it would be nice if the footstep audio effect did the same thing. Some pans just come as standard with edit software and will allow left to right or right to left to be adjusted by keyframes. If you don't have this facility, there are manual ways of doing it by razoring up the audio and applying different levels of audio to the left and right channels. Looking at this scene, there are footsteps when the bobby is out of frame (right), three shots of him on screen and footsteps again with him out of frame (left). Finding the central position for the bobby (i.e. where he is in front of the subject) will give you the centre position of the sound. Razoring half a second either side of this line means that central track values are, by default, applied to this clip, which should be kept as it is. It's the rest of the audio that needs changing.

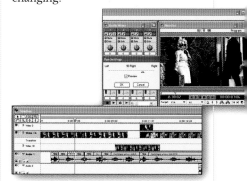

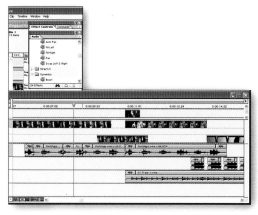

We go to the start of the action, where the bobby's off screen, and use the *Razor* on the track to make a new clip to the right. This next clip is given an audio pan value between

the central and right speaker.
The central section is left free of
effect, then the other razored clips
are treated with *Pan* values between
the centre and left speakers...

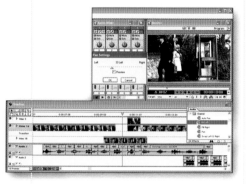

...until the footsteps effect fills the
left speaker and the volume slowly
dies away.

Razoring up these different shots
allows for different values of track
output to be applied to all of them.

This is the premix finesse. Before
you throw yourself into the mix,
though, listen to the whole of your
scene again. Is there a word lost on
a music beat? An effect that's so
quiet that it sounds like someone
dropped a mic on set? In fact,
anything that sounds like an
accident has to be dealt with,
whether you decide to amplify one
clip or dampen another.

The master mix

Your master audio mix concerns the
levels of audio between tracks and
how they interact with each other.
This can either be done through
your volume levels on the *Timeline*,
or through the audio mixer (if your
software has one).

Consider your genre. If it's
comedy, an effects track tends to be
slightly louder; if it's a musical
interlude, the music track needs to
be amplified; if it's a dramatic scene,
the dialogue track is the most
important. The reason you need
good-quality speakers in your edit is
that your playback source will be
completely different. You need the
best mix that you can in order that
you don't lose out later – and there's

certainly no point in fiddling around
with stereo or quadraphonic mixes
in the edit if it's unlikely that it'll
ever be heard that way.

When you are listening to the
whole of your sound, mix it the way
that you want it. Audio is an effect
all of its own and it can excuse
video, enhance video and get an
audience on side – excited even.
The one thing to remember while
getting your levels right, though, is
never to exceed 0Db. Digital audio
becomes a horrific experience over
that level, so keep your highest
levelled track at 0 and adjust
everything else to suit.

distribution

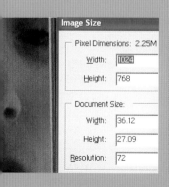
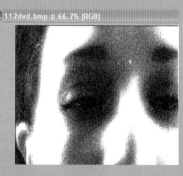
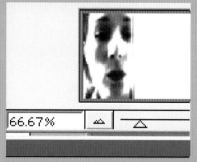

Introduction

Rendering and exporting individual scenes or entire movie timelines can be extremely satisfying and rewarding – and it can be mind-numbing and frustrating. Longer timelines – especially those with effects, colour correction and complicated transitions – take much longer to render. That's because your computer is creating a brand new file that combines all the information on the timeline.

Exporting back to tape is another option, but only if you have a DV input on your camera. Depending on your software and camera, you may need to press record manually, but most of the time it can all be done automatically via FireWire. Make sure that you're not right at the start of the tape beforehand, by recording 30 seconds of black before the movie begins. This avoids using the most vulnerable part of the tape.

Exporting individual scenes can be very useful for an editor. Not only do they provide a reference for what has already been cut (good housekeeping), but they can be graded to maintain consistency of colour and tone in their entirety.

Exporting can only be undertaken once the whole timeline is rendered, and your edit software will automatically do this for you once you've clicked to export. You do have some options here, and finding the most suitable file format to export as is crucial. It all depends on what you intend to do with the scene or movie.

If it's a scene that you're going to export, so that you can edit it against other scenes, make sure that you're consistent when it comes to file formats. AVIs are usually the format of preference here, as they have minimal compression and both Macs and PCs can handle them within an edit environment. As a rule here, however, you want to save in the same format that you've already been editing your clips with.

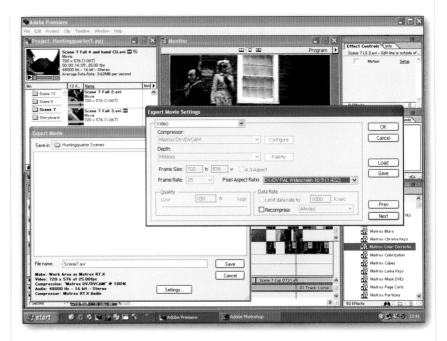

Your computer editing software will have presets for the format that you've chosen. Always check the settings to ensure that you've got the right standard (NTSC or PAL) and the right ratio (4:3 or 16: 9).

If it's a whole movie that you want to export, your means of distribution will have a major impact on how you do it. DVD, for example, uses MPEG-2, a standard that heavily compresses the data.

Export settings in Adobe Premiere. You will have presets to help, but make sure that the standard and aspect ratio are correct before you start the process off.

If you use a Mac, you might use the QuickTime .MOV format instead (it works with PCs too). You need to watch the settings, however, or the format's high compression rate can affect image quality.

The last base option is to stream your movie over the Internet. This is very particular and relies on finding the best balance between image quality and speed of delivery (*see page 134-135*).

Compression is where it's at when it comes to exporting. The sophistication of your export codec will dictate just how good your image and how small the file size will be. The better the codec is, the better your image will play out when decompressed. If you're exporting to DV tape, however, you won't suffer any image loss at all: DV tape (including MiniDV) is the one format that can handle the

48Khz, 16-bit, CD-quality audio is the least your Hollywood movie deserves. Set the *Interleave* value to *1 frame* if your movie has dialogue.

Your export settings will depend on your editing software and the hardware in your system. This PC uses a Matrox video card, which uses with its own specialist codec.

massive amounts of information without needing to compress it first. Your hardware and software will have their own preferred codecs and it's wise to go with them. These will be the ones you used when

capturing, and should mean your movie goes out in the same excellent state it came in. For the best audio, always stick with 16-bit 48/44KHz data and sample rate. This is CD quality and should be set automatically. If you have an interleave value option – a synchronized link between audio and video – then this should be set to every frame, especially for a movie with dialogue.

Exporting to .AVI or .MOV format isn't complicated unless you give your movie different settings than those that you conducted the edit with. If you wish to export to DVD or a webstream, then things start to get more tricky.

Make Your Own DVDs

One reason why the DVD format is so popular is that it fits high quality video and audio onto a single silver disk. It's all down to MPEG-2 compression. The MPEG-2 standard uses smart algorithms to work out the difference between one frame and the last, and then changes only whatever data needs to be changed in order to keep the moving image running smoothly.

Any digital media format has a bitrate – the quantity of data that is handled every second when the format is decompressed and played. MPEG-2 uses a variable bitrate. The algorithm adjusts to create low bitrates between frames that don't change much and high bitrates for those that do. It then makes calculations based on the runtime of the movie to store enough data to ensure smooth viewing.

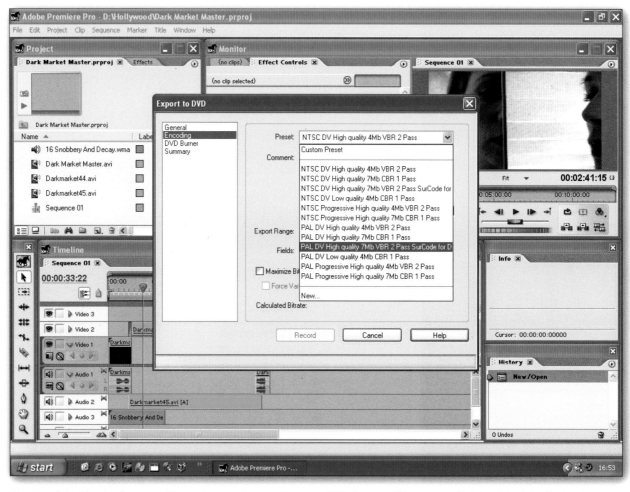

Check and double-check your settings when you're encoding your DVD. Some settings can switch back to defaults, leaving your movie in the wrong standard or the wrong ratio.

Why do you need to know this? Because it's important to set your variable bitrate low when you're exporting to DVD. This not only means that you can get more on your disk – especially if your movie is approaching feature length – but it will have more chance of playing on domestic DVD players. Your edit software might make the adjustment itself by calculating the data in the project, but there are bitrate calculators online if you need one.

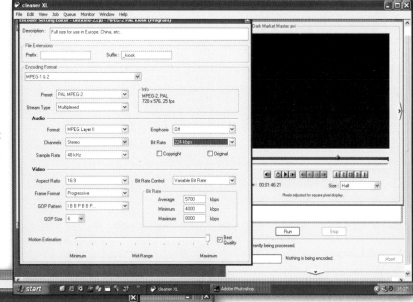

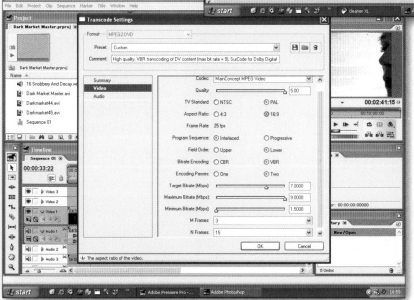

When you are exporting to MPEG-2, you also need to make sure that all the rest of your settings are still correct. If it's edit software that is doing the encoding, then it might well default to standard values when you change the format from .AVI. Most importantly, it's your standard and your ratio that need checking.

Above and right: Relying on your editing application to transcode from DV to MPEG-2 might not get you the best results from your DVD. If you've got money to burn, industry-spec applications, such as Cleaner XL, will optimize your MPEG-2 movie.

If you're encoding from within your editing software, you may not have the variety of options that you want. Transcoding (copying from one format to another) is not usually the most effective way of getting your MPEG at its best. It might be a better approach to take an .AVI into a specialized cleaner package. You probably can't afford an industry

standard package such as Discreet's Cleaner XL, but other packages can convert and clean up your video without costing the Earth and without losing image quality in the process.

Again, if you do have the options there, it's not just the visuals that you might want to filter. Certainly, some cleaners can give a better quality broadcast output (using more intricate data-processing) than your edit software will.

With any encoder, don't be afraid to try different settings and try the results on a home DVD player. Experiment with a shot clip; make notes; watch it; do it again...

Of course, encoding is one thing; making it look like a Hollywood movie experience in a glitzy case on a shelf is another. And that bit is just a little more fun.

DVD menu design

There are several software packages out there that will let you make your own Hollywood DVD. Not only are they designed to produce something of which you can be proud, but the more substantial applications contain encoders with presets that won't give you a settings migraine.

They do what they say on the box, and help you to create strong DVD menus, usually consisting of four major visual elements: your movie, a background image, text and a set of interactive buttons. Don't be arbitrary about design. It may not be your strong point, but branding your movie doesn't have to be complicated – in fact, the simpler and more focussed it is, the better your branding will be.

Use the font that you used for your title sequence for the title menu; use an enticing or globally representative still from your movie as a background; use a stark, vivid

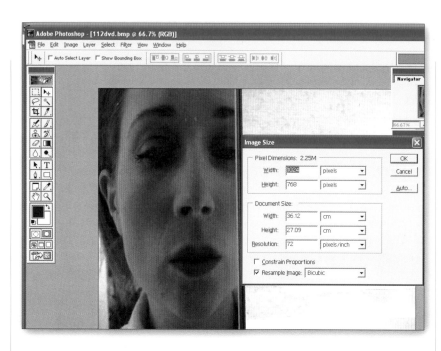

still as a button. Most interfaces can cope with JPEGs, BMPs, TGAs or any other graphics file that you want to use. If you find yourself unable to grab stills of the frame you want in your edit software, open the movie, grab the screen as a still image and copy it into a graphics program.

If you've invested in more expensive DVD software, you'll want to find even more graphics for chapter stops and submenus. This is another purpose for your production stills – give the audience something they won't see in the movie.

DVD presentation is all about wrapping the movie up and putting it to bed. If you think you've got a bit of time to spare, throw in a diary or gag reel from production. The further you go with this, the more complete the DVD and the more it will form an entire experience. Unlike a credit sequence, you don't need to be concerned about appearing gratuitous. Submenus are there to find if you want to search

If your graphics application doesn't contain a range of DV-friendly presets, you can always change the settings by hand.

Use the *De-interlace* filter to remove any horrible artefacts from your pristine still frame.

for them, and there are some people out there that want to see how bad your storyboards are.

If you are taking movie grabs to your DVD authoring software, make sure that you're taking them across at the right ratio and resolution. Photoshop has presets to cover most digital video formats, and a

De-interlace filter to avoid the unsightly double image of video stills. The difference between odd and even fields can sometimes define the difference between a wry smile and a stupid grin, so choose what works best for your image.

Adding effects to the shot to match the style of the menu is child's play to a graphics application...

...importing it into your authoring software will help you on the road to strong branding.

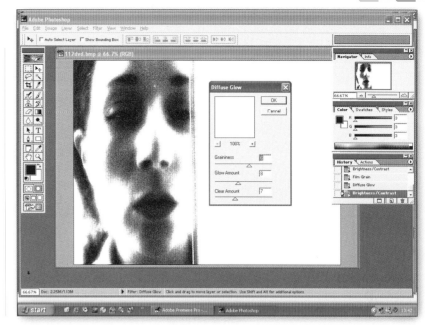

Online Movies

One of the most viable ways of opening up your market and potential audience is to put your movie online. This is where your movie becomes a balancing act, with you juggling quality against download speeds. First off, though, there are some essentials that you'll need to bear in mind if you want to share your movie with the world.

Your finished Hollywood movie is a large file full of complicated digital data—and that's something that the Internet still hasn't learned to deal with properly. Even with broadband and a large bandwidth at your end, your end user may well be sitting in front of their Jurassic PC with a 56K modem plugged into their phone line. That's why you need to make decisions that affect the quality of your movie, or small compromises to split your audience. Providing three different versions of your movie—one for 56K, one for 300K cable, and one for broadband—can help you reach out to everyone.

As an uncompressed file, every four and half minutes of video with audio is 1Gb heavy. To a viewer with a 56K modem, 1Gb will take 17 or 18 hours to download. Get the picture? They won't, unless you compress it first.

You may already have encoded and compressed your movie for DVD, but even MPEG-2 isn't going to cut the mustard here. Reducing the frame size, reducing the number of pixels (resolution) and reducing the number of frames per second will all help lowering the final file

size, and there are three main formats that can help: Windows Media, QuickTime and RealMedia. Which one should you use? Well, it depends on a few realities.

The first is that while QuickTime files and RealMedia files are cross-platform, the Windows Media format often sends Mac users scurrying to a Windows site for a software download. Anything that makes your movie a hassle to watch will not entice an audience to watch it.

The second reality is that QuickTime and Windows Media are very good at showing short videos while maintaining quality. Anything pushing twenty minutes will be much better off as a RealMedia file, but the image quality is nowhere near as good.

Lastly, if you have a separate encoder or cleaner, you should use it to export instead of your edit software. It is very likely to have fewer presets and more options for manually tweaking the balance between quality and speed.

It's worth trying out different settings on a sample of your movie and viewing them after encoding. Compression will affect your movie

differently depending on how it has been shot and edited. One effect will be to reduce the number of frames per second, and if you have a lot of fast motion in your shots, this will give your movie a heavily animated look. This can be adjusted by the Sample Rate, and if you do have action sequences, it's better to keep this at the higher end of the scale and take a blow elsewhere.

Elsewhere might be in the resolution or image size, but if you've got a lot of detail or long shots then this may not be the sacrifice that you want. What you can live with instead is a loss of true chrominance and luminance. Compression can round off your carefully controlled colours and apply a rougher web palette, changing luminance values as it goes. Certainly, you won't have as much contrast as you once did.

Compression also relies on similarities between frames to make calculations. If a background doesn't change, the information doesn't have to be resampled, and this saves your audience a load of download time. Again, fast action causes problems as the image is always changing.

Finally, get a good server. There are more and more out there that deal specifically with delivering video, with enough bandwidth to save a bit more of your quality. Servers will either stream progressively by delivering packets of information to a temporary folder, so the player application plays one packet while downloading the next – or the user can simply download the entire media file. Media downloads allow you to put your movie on a server in most formats (AVI, MPEG, etc) and these are saved to the hard drive of your audience's computers, which may or may not be a good thing.

Both of these methods use either constant bitrates or variable bitrates. Because your Hollywood movie is likely to contain scenes of differing complexity of video and audio, a variable bitrate is the better option, taking the time saved in simpler scenes and distributing it to the more complicated to maintain speed.

That just leaves audio. Cutting audio to 22KHz won't change it terribly noticeably to an audience's usual slack PC audio setup, so go ahead if you feel the need.

The audience is waiting...

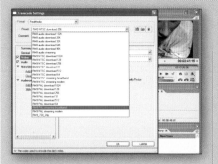

QuickTime, Windows Media and RealMedia are all subject to constant upgrades. Make sure that you check that your export is being transcoded to the latest version. These presets offer the past two versions of RealMedia. Selecting the broadband version limits the audience, but it allows those with a faster connection to view your movie in the way you intended. The numbers here refer to the bandwidth that the video will take up while streaming.

The presets can choose the audience. Decide what connection they are most likely to have, and make your choices accordingly. Try to reach a balance between accessibility and quality.

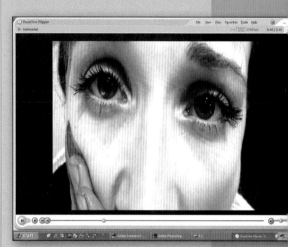

The final output in RealMedia is one that copes a lot better with close-ups and static shots...

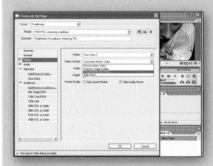

Presets help you look beyond the numbers. This movie contains a lot of running around, so *Smoothest Motion Video* wins out over *Sharpest Image Quality*. From here, there's a choice of resizing for high speed or high quality. RealMedia wants to offer 4:3 as 320x240 pixels, which means that sticking to a height of 240 pixels will cause the width to need adjusting to 426 pixels.

...than it does with the action sequences.

hollywood tricks

Introduction

You might not have a Hollywood budget to play with, but that doesn't mean your movie has to look cheap. Think creatively and make the most of your digital tools.

Having the right equipment as you shoot will help you make your Hollywood movie, but if you don't have the means or the budget, you can usually find a way around.

Actors moving around a set, spouting lines, being tracked by cameras, cables, and mics is the practical side of moviemaking. Setting them in a world of believable artifice is where you can start raising your production values. It's the little things in life that make the movie believable in that environment. Even if a set, an effect, a stunt – whatever – looks insurmountable on the page, it's always possible to make an audience believe.

To make them believe, it's not necessarily a question of showing them with vivid visuals. The schools of thought concerning 'more is more' and 'less is more' usually refer to explicitness within the horror and thriller genres. There is no right or wrong. The overt cannibalism of *Dawn Of The Dead* doesn't make it a cheaper movie than the sublime discretion of *Parents*; the explicit sex in *Basic Instinct* doesn't make its love scenes any more believable than their modest equivalents in *The Big Easy*. It's simply how the moviemaker decides to phrase their movie. It's all about what you want, what you can afford and what the actors can do.

Another example: Bruce the shark from *Jaws*. It doesn't function properly on set, so the POV of the shark through water and breaking

the surface is used. As long as you can get around or work within your time and budget and qualify what you are doing to an audience, your movie will be watertight. A badly-handled effect can be every bit as disappointing as a no-show from an expensive and impossible monster. Either of these two situations can pull an audience back from believing in your movie.

It's you who decided what to show an audience and what not to show them. You decide where you want them to look in frame, what you want them to imagine and what you want them to believe. A lot of this can be done in the edit, but some of it needs to be done while you're shooting.

Controlling your set runs to every element of moviemaking. From the practicalities of taping cables and hiding mics, to the feeding and starvation of the camera with light, always make sure that no matter what the issue is, you're prepared. Make sure that you're carrying gaffer tape, black and white card stock and as much forethought as you can garner. The quality of the performances, the audio, and the video – and so your production values – depend on this control.

Digital video does offer up some more possibilities, however. With the right know-how, you can make an audience believe that your main character can become a werewolf, or that it is snowing at Christmas. All a

Harness the power of your editing software, and you can raise production values using built-in effects and compositing tools.

lot of these effects need is a setup in themselves, or some thought during the shoot or the edit.

The fact is that there is always a solution to anything beyond your time and budget. The location can always be changed, the budget stretched, the shot can be tighter, you can use a cutaway, make reference in the dialogue – anything to make an audience believe.

If a piece of equipment is worthwhile and you might use it again, invest from the start. It doesn't even need to be a huge investment. A bluescreen or greenscreen is a worthy example – and once you've got one and used it, you probably won't look back.

The cheap option is to buy a length of blue or green material. Always use felt as it doesn't reflect the light. Lighting material can be a royal pain when there are creases – and therefore shadows – in it. This is the reason why these spring-loaded, taut chromakey backgrounds are

available for purchase. In the right contexts, using chromakey allows you to perform effects and go the extra mile to make your audience believe in your movie.

It's not just effects, though, that create the real world of your movie. The details that you don't really notice, and that pass an audience by, are the things that stop them believing if you get them wrong.

These things concern your art department. If you think, having had one movie's headaches, that you can continue making more, then hold on to that leftover make-up, wardrobe and prop bag. It contains stuff that you can use again and again.

Remember – you're not alone. Everyone has 'things', and you know enough people who have them to make your Hollywood movie. They want you to make it too, so don't be coy. It's beg, borrow and steal time. Above all, be prepared to use something different than you imagined and make it work for you.

How to Make a Bluescreen

Whether you want to fly your actors through the air, send them to the future or make objects hover in the air, it's easy to create amazing effects with a bluescreen. Film an object or person in front of a bluescreen, and you can use your editing software to remove the background with a keying filter. You can then place any image or footage that you like behind them.

1 You can easily build a frame from four pieces of wood nailed together. If you prefer, you can buy a cheap old painting and use the frame. Stretch a bed sheet tightly across the frame, and nail it into place so that there are no creases. Don't use a sheet with patterns, or they will show up through the paint.

2 Buy one or two small pots of light, bright blue paint. You may want to put an undercoat of dark blue paint on first.

3 The top coat of paint should be applied all in one go, to avoid areas drying at different rates. You may find that the material sags slightly, but it will tighten again as the paint dries.

4 Use a small brush, and make sure no hairs fall out and stick to the screen. If they do, remove them, or they will cast tiny shadows that make the keying work difficult. Paint vertically, then horizontally, to reduce the appearance of brush marks.

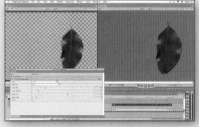

6 Let's try it out. Film an object in front of the screen (here we've used a leaf suspended by a piece of thread). Now load the shot into your computer and apply the *Bluescreen* or *Chromakey* filter, and adjust the sliders until all the blue vanishes.

7 Now drag a clip of background footage to the timeline, and place it beneath your leaf shot. The leaf will appear to be floating in midair. If this were a real shot, the distant background would be blurred, so apply a *Blur* effect to the lower layer.

5 Leave your bluescreen to dry thoroughly before testing it, or it will change colour as you work, making the keying almost impossible. Before using it on an important job, try it out to make sure the colour is even, and easily removed by the computer.

BLUE OR GREEN

It's now common Hollywood practice to use a greenscreen instead of blue. It's a good idea if your actor has blue eyes or clothes; otherwise the software will remove the eyes and clothes from the shot. When your actors wear green, use a bluescreen. Never use a bluescreen if you are lighting the scene with sunlight. Cameras see sunlight as slightly blue, and when you use your software to remove the bluescreen the sunlight will disappear, along with most of your actor's face. A bluescreen is best used in scenes shot indoors with artificial light.

142 How to Use Chromakey

Chromakey is an easy way to create stunning visual effects or achieve shots that would be otherwise impossible. You shoot in front of a bluescreen, then use a *Chromakey* filter to remove the blue. This enables you to shoot in a safe, controlled environment, with no weather problems, then place the actor in a harsh or fantasy landscape, or in distant locations shot at a completely different time. If you change your mind about which background you want to appear behind your actor, it can be changed in postproduction later.

2 Apply the *Chromakey* filter, or the *Bluescreen* filter – different packages call it different things. Adjust the Tolerance levels until the blue has almost vanished. In Final Cut Express or Final Cut Pro, you can remove the blue line around your actor by increasing *Edge Thinning* and *Softening*. A *Blue Spill* filter will get rid of any remaining. It takes time to find the correct balance, but when you're done there should be no blue around the actor, nor should the edges of your actor be transparent.

1 Shoot your actor in front of a bluescreen, or a coloured wall. Make sure no shadows fall on the bluescreen by putting your lights high up. Keep your actor a good distance from the screen, to avoid picking up blue light which could ruin the shot. If you want to show your actor's feet, make sure that the floor is also painted blue.

3 Place your background footage in a layer beneath your actor's clip. Your actor will probably appear to be stuck onto the background footage, so apply a *Color Correction* filter, and adjust the foreground to match the background.

4 The finished composite is more realistic if you allow the background to be slightly blurred with a *Blur* filter (the *Gaussian Blur* if your application has one). Watch the entire clip to ensure that your *Chromakey* filter works throughout.

6 If you want to see your actor's face front-on in a car scene, shoot in a garage, making sure you block out all daylight. Even a small bluescreen placed outside the rear window will create good results. Make sure it's evenly lit.

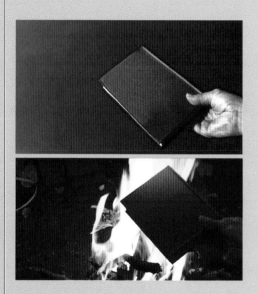

7 Shoot your moving background footage with the same zoom setting on the camera, so that the two shots blend together well. The result should be very convincing.

5 Chromakey can be used to avoid putting your actor in danger. If you want your actor to place something in a fire, shoot the fire, and then shoot the actor's hand in front of a bluescreen. When composited together, the result doesn't even appear to be a special effect.

BACKGROUND PLANS

Although chromakey gives you great flexibility, planning ahead will help make the final shot more believable. It helps if you shoot your background footage first, so that you can show the actor what environment to imagine. You should also try to recreate the light from the background scene in terms of softness and direction, but don't worry about matching the colour until postproduction.

How to Use Smoke

One of the best ways to add a professional atmosphere to your work is through the use of smoke. An inexpensive smoke machine from a party hire shop, can give you Hollywood-style lighting for a fraction of the price. Smoke is used by many leading directors, including Steven Spielberg and Ridley Scott, to add volume to light. Although this is not a naturalistic look, it helps to make any space feel more film-like than a standard room.

1 The technique is known as backlighting, because the light comes from the rear of the scene, and points towards the camera. The lamp itself doesn't have to be in shot (and usually shouldn't be), but unless light comes towards the camera, the smoke won't show up as anything other than haze. When light is aimed towards the camera, smoky light beams show up. The darker the room, the greater the effect.

2 When you first fill a room with smoke it will be very uneven, so use boards to waft the smoke around. Evenly spread smoke looks like thick light, whereas uneven smoke looks like smoke, and you don't want the audience to actually think there's smoke in the room. You are simply trying to create the effect of thick beams of light.

3 You can take advantage of sunlight coming through a window, to add smoky backlighting. This can help to draw attention to your actor, rather than having the audience focus on the room your actor is in.

4 Coloured lights will create coloured smoke, and this will have a strong influence on the atmosphere of the scene. Yellow or brown can give you an underground feel, while green is good for an alien or evil atmosphere.

5 Place a light directly behind your actor, pointing straight at the camera, and you will create a dramatic image, with light beams shooting out around the actor. This is such a powerful effect it is best reserved for supernatural moments.

6 If you're shooting on location smoke can still work well, so long as there is good lighting contrast. You'll need to use more smoke, and shoot as fast as possible, because the slightest breeze will clear the air rapidly.

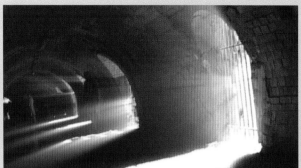

7 Simulated fire can be created by pumping smoke through the remains of a bonfire. You need to position the cameras so that the smoke is between your position and the sun, or the smoke will appear to be a red haze.

SIDE EFFECTS

Actors can be uncomfortable around smoke, assuming that it may have an effect on their vocal chords. Reassure them that this isn't the case, but do be aware that blasting smoke right around an actor can be distracting. If you're shooting an emotional moment you should blast the smoke before the actor takes up position. Smoke machines often cough a few seconds after you've switched them off, so when you've distributed the smoke, move the machine into another room before calling action.

146 How to Shoot Underwater

Shooting underwater is one of the most dangerous and difficult tasks for a film crew, but the good news is you can create great results in your living room. Many directors believe that fake shots look more impressive, because they can be be lit more accurately and controlled down to the last detail. By shooting in your homemade studio, and using software to finish the job, there are no risks and the results look fantastic.

SMOKE

You may want a darker, murkier effect, as though a scuba diver is searching the ocean floor. Shoot in a dark room, making sure no light hits the wall behind the actor. Fill the room with smoke by burning lots of incense, and have the actor point a torch through the smoke. When composited into an underwater scene, this smoky beam of light will recreate the effect of an underwater torch.

1 Shoot your actor lying down against a blue background. You can use your bluescreen, but your actor may find it easier if you cover a couch with blue cloth. Make sure that hair flows upwards and away from the actor. You can even use a hairdryer to add to this effect, so long as you keep it out of the actor's eyes.

2 For background ocean footage, go to the nearest aquarium and get some shots of the biggest tanks. Be careful to avoid reflections on the glass. If there are no large aquariums, close-ups of a regular fish tank will often suffice.

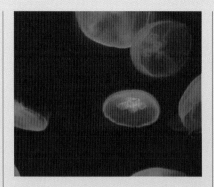

3 While at the aquarium, find a tank with fish that appear bright against a dark background. These can be added in front of your actor, so it's best if they are semi-transparent, as with jellyfish.

4 In your editing software use the *Chromakey* filter to remove the blue background from behind your actor, making sure the flowing hair is still visible. Drop the ocean layer behind the actor, and put the jellyfish layer in front. By sandwiching the actor you create a more believable sense of depth.

5 The result looks best if you apply a *Color Correction* filter to the actor's layer, and shift it towards blue. A slight Blur will also add to the sense of underwater murkiness.

6 By shooting from unusual angles, you can create interesting results. Visualize the finished look when you are shooting.

7 Although your actor will be lying down, the finished shot will give the impression that she is standing upright on the bottom of the ocean.

How to Create Gunshots

Whether you are shooting an old-fashioned Western or a *Matrix*-style movie, you will want your gunshots to show up. A realistic gunshot is a combination of sound, movement, a flash of light at the gun's muzzle and a spark where the bullet hits. You can create the gunshot safely in the computer, without the need for complex setups. This saves time and money, without the need for risky explosives or expensive replica guns. Inform the local police of your intentions if you're shooting where others might see you.

1 If you're using accurate gun replicas you may need a licence, depending on local laws. A toy gun looks just as good, so long as your actor can make it appear heavy. Try filling the gun with modelling clay to give it more weight. When the actor fires a shot, the gun should tilt upwards, followed by a recoil in the arm.

2 We'll create the blast effect seperately. Set up your camera in a darkened room, and insert a drinking straw into a bag of flour, pushing a small plug of flour into one end. Blow the flour out of the straw and film the result. Your lamp should be in front of the camera, out of shot, but shining through the flour.

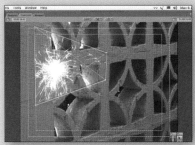

6 You can use the sparkler footage from the Explosion tutorial (see page 151) to create a bullet impact. Add the footage, reduce its *Opacity*, and use the *Perspective* tool to drag the edges of the layer until it matches the perspective of the wall.

3 Use your editing software to layer the flour-shot over the muzzle. In Final Cut Express, the *Add Composite* mode makes the flour look like a flash (use your program's equivalent). You might also need to use a garbage matte to cut out the edges of the layer.

5 When the angle of the gun changes, shoot the flour from the relevant angle. To avoid getting flour on the lens, keep the camera a good distance away and zoom in.

7 The beauty of this technique is that you can easily add several impacts to one image, so long as you add sufficient sound effects. For added realism, insert another sparkler layer, but change the *Composite Mode* to *Subtract* or *Multiply*. This makes it look like a cloud of dust or dirt is being thrown off by the surface.

4 You can download gun sounds from the net, and add them to your footage. The finished result will look best if it lasts for no more than three or four frames.

BLOOD

If you want a character to be shot, the easiest way is to show a close-up of your actor at moment of impact, with a trickle of blood seeping out of the mouth. You can then cut to a wide shot, and show the wound. If you want to see the bullet hit and create the wound in real time, fill a wide tube with a mixture of wet cotton wool, corn syrup and red food colouring. Blow this at the character's chest as hard as you can. If it's blown out fast enough, the impact will look as though blood is exploding from within. Practice this many times, before using it on set.

How to Fake Wounds

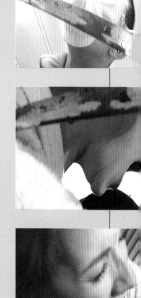

Cuts and stabs can appear in any genre. In romantic comedy, they can introduce a nurse and patient – but they're more usually found in horror, as a mark of the heroine's peril, or an end to another whining teenager.

Whatever way you need to use blood, don't use the real thing. It's not that actors mind if you cut them up a bit, but blood and offal from the local butcher soon smell rotten under lights.

Theatrical and joke shops stock fake blood. It can be quite expensive if you want a lot – and it's easy to make if you know how.

1 To make your own fake blood, use corn syrup with cochineal. Don't just use red colouring; blue and yellow are the other important primaries that give it that extra bit of realism. If it's fresh and arterial, try a bit more blue that you feel comfortable with; if the blood's supposed to be old, put a bit more yellow in the mix.

2 When applying blood to your actors, try and pad them out and cover the set as much as you can. It tends to get everywhere. If you've made your own, it can be sticky and it's not an altogether comfortable nor convenient experience for anybody. Worse, any colouring will stain the skin of your actors, something that isn't useful for a second take or going into a different scene. To combat this, use methylated spirits to get rid of any stains, or give the actor a thin layer of PVA glue before application so that they can rub the whole thing off at the end.

3 This simple sequence is only made convincing by the camerawork (edgy), framing (concealing) and acting (terrified). These are the core essentials of believing any special effect. The 'less is more' school will tell you that it's far more effective, but here it's a time and budget decision. Looking at the setup frame by frame, there's the end of a plastic knife, a bit of blood and a screaming girl trying to keep the door closed. When it runs, it's a reasonably convincing prelude...

If you want to see the effect of a knife cutting skin, however, you have two choices. Both of them require one element to be bogus. One is a simple tubed blade from a theatrical shop that squirts blood out along the edge of a rubber or plastic knife. This won't give you the effect of actual skin-cutting, though, and that is where you might try your hand at prosthetics.

6 Filling a balloon with the fake blood and pushing it underneath the thin latex then allows for the blood to flow when punctured.

4 Prosthetics at their base level, are latex applications that are designed to be glued with mastic onto the skin. These are either created as deformities, or as part of the actor under which there is a fake blood release. When you use prosthetics, the challenge is to try and blend them into your subject.

5 In this case, a makeup blending to the skin is eschewed in favour of hiding the edge of the prosthetic with the bathrobe. A rip is torn conveniently for the knife but not taped back up. An audience knows that a knife will rip a bathrobe quite easily; showing the knife, showing the bathrobe, and showing the cutaway of the victim's expression will fill in the rest without having the complication of another layer to cut through. If this was required, Velcro or surgical tape would hold the robe together.

7 The rest of it is all in the acting, framing and in the editing. Remember, you don't need to take it fast if you're shooting, as you can add pace in the edit...

How to Shoot a Fight Scene

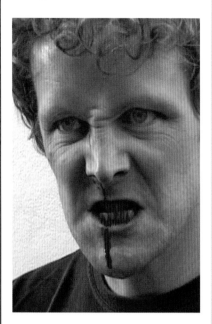

There's no such thing as an action movie without a fight scene, and you even see fights in art movies and romantic comedies. The basic tricks are nearly a hundred years old, but still look believable on screen. Your actors don't need any training, just very careful rehearsal and the judgement to throw a punch off target. Film no more than a punch or two at a time, then cut them together for the final film.

1 Your actors should always know who is going to punch, and where. There should never be any surprises, which is why planning and slow motion rehearsal are important. The actor throwing the punch should pull one arm back, to indicate where the punch is coming from. This movement will be cut out during the edit, but it helps your actors know what to expect. The punch itself should fly past the victim's face. Practice to get the timing of the head pullback just right.

2 The same over-the-shoulder setup can be used for the reverse punch. Again, the fist should curve around in front of the face. So long as the actors time it well, the impact should look fairly convincing.

3 A real punch in the stomach is devastating, but for the screen your punching actor needn't make full contact. Instead, the victim should leap backward and up, to make it look like the punch has hit its mark. Timing is everything, so practice, practice, practice.

6 When shooting the stomach punch from a wide angle, the victim can leap quite a long way in the air. On its own, this shot may look unconvincing, so cut it together with the close-up for maximum impact.

4 In wide shots, your actors need to exaggerate body movement even more, or the punches will look like they are having no effect. A fist that goes right past an actor's head will appear to be making painful contact if timed correctly.

5 You don't need to be too precise. Even punches that miss wildly will look good if the victim twists away from the punch forcefully enough.

7 Fake blood can easily be made by mixing food colouring with corn syrup. This can then be trickled down the nose and into the teeth. If the fight continues from this point, put some blood on the opponent's knuckles as well.

PUNCH SOUNDS

There are two approaches to punch sounds in film. The most common is to use a huge sound, almost like a car door being slammed. Although unrealistic, audiences accept this convention as being believable. The other approach is a more realistic slapping thud. Record the sound of a cabbage being punched, and you'll get the right effect. Choose the approach that best suits the style of your project, and don't forget to record the sound of actors' feet shuffling, and their breath. It all adds to the final result.

How to Shoot a Car Chase

A good car chase raises tension levels, and provides on-screen drama. If you have an unlimited budget you can close roads and hire stunt drivers, but it's often easier to fake a car chase with careful filming and editing. By combining simple shots in dramatic ways, with screeching tires and roaring engines, you can create the impression of crazed driving without ever going over the speed limit.

1 The classic car-chase shot is taken from the side, looking directly at the driver. You can shoot this from the passenger seat with a handheld camera. If you want more stability it only takes a few minutes to set up your tripod in the car. The background scenery blurs superbly from this angle, making the car appear to be going about three times faster than it's actually travelling.

2 Shoot the driver's hands when going around corners. Fast drivers move their hands smoothly, so don't ask your actors to strain at the wheel. Just let them corner normally. By showing brief moments of wheel-turning, you'll create the impression of the car screaming into corners. The background scenery swings past dramatically when going around corners.

3 Put your camera on a tripod and shoot the cars going past. For the best sense of speed, don't move the camera, so that the cars flash in out of frame in a blur. If you want to show more of the car, follow it for a short while, then let it rush out of frame as though you can't keep up.

5 When you're on a piece of open road, get your actor to drive as fast as is safe and legal, and use a short lens to make the scenery rush past in a blur.

6 Make sure you shoot both drivers, to give a sense of the chase. Shots of actors can be far longer than shots of the car or the road.

7 Shoot lots of close-up cutaways, which can be inserted into the action, to create the sense of speed and motion.

4 Shooting from the back seat helps the audience see the car that's being chased, but don't linger on these shots, or the lack of real speed will be obvious. Add tyre screeches (downloaded from the net) when you edit, and it will appear to be a high-speed chase.

TOW TRUCK

Actors find car chases difficult to shoot, not least because they have to drive safely while appearing to drive dangerously. A solution is to put the car on a trailer, which is then towed behind another vehicle. This lets your actor concentrate on their facial expressions without the risk of running off the road. If you want to film dialogue during a car chase, always use a trailer, otherwise the actors will hold back their performance while concentrating on the road.

156 How to Shoot Flashbacks

Messing with the minds of characters is a very old Hollywood device - one sometimes undertaken to further the story, or one that's sometimes designed to trick an audience. A flashback can be an easy way of giving a character history, or a device to motivate revenge, or provide concealed information to add excitement to a film's denouement.

2 Inserting the shot next to the character pre-action sequence looking into the mirror provides the reverse shot: the viewer is told that she is looking back at a bloodied version of herself. At this point they ask the question: Why?

Alternatively, Hollywood might use a dream sequence – this might provide a quick shock, a psychological dimension or even a vital clue that helps solve a mystery. The big difference between the two is that dream sequences often contain something illogical – a clash of time and place or a different feel that signals that what you're watching isn't the 'real' narrative.

Occasionally, flashbacks and dreams trick the audience – they won't be shot, acted or even edited any differently from the real story, and their nature is only revealed at the end of the sequence. Otherwise, they're usually treated in some way to inform an audience. The decision that you make will depend on the style of your movie.

1 To inform an audience, always start with the character's eyes. They're the gateway to the mind, which is the playground for what is to follow. If this horror sequence were to work as a flashback, taking the end shot of the character wiping blood onto her face to the beginning of the sequence subverts the natural chronology. To an audience, though, it is shockingly bad continuity unless they're given more information in movie language to allow them to understand.

3 Reversing the shot begins to give a viewer a bit more information. Because the shot has the benefit of an absolute change in the character's look (i.e. she has blood on her), it's obviously not a continuity error. Turning the shot around so that her actions look slightly reversed (the blood is wiped completely from her face) and slowing the shot down to make it more apparent, allows the audience enough time and information to know that there is a change in time – because the place is the same.

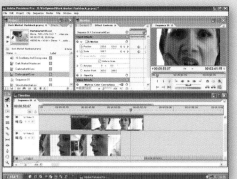

4 Because this is showing an audience the aftereffects of something that has happened, it's a flashback. To enable the action sequence to be in the past, it needs to be applied in such a way that anything following is regarded as the past. Using a motion control, pushing into the character's eyes tells the audience that we are moving into her space and perception: her mind.

6 Alternatively less flashy and – today – a bit more classy, a dissolve will do the same thing.

5 From here, there are two possible transitions to the past. One is the device of yore, the video transition. The most clichéd of these, damned to the vaults of movie language, is a ripple. These generally take an audience back to a place that is the calm before the storm.

7 A more modern transition, though, is not to have one at all. Cutting straight to the action – in this case, the killer trying to get through the door – is disorienting for the audience, and that keeps you one step ahead if you want to shock them.

8 Simply carrying on the flashback to its conclusion forces you to come back to your subject. It's incredibly important to top and tail a flashback sequence. If you don't, you can really confuse and annoy them. Get them back to the space and time of the movie in the same way that you went in: a transition or a meaningful cut to the subject's eyes. In this case, the subject's scream in the video and audio crossfades back to a more searching mirror image.

HOLLYWOOD TRICKS

How to Create a Clone

With the help of editing software, you can give your actor an identical twin on screen. By shooting two versions of the scene and combining them, you can even get your actor to interact with themselves. This special effect is now used so often in film and television that it's almost taken for granted. However, while splitting the screen is simple, for the best effect you'll want your cloned actors to talk or pass items between one another. Here, your actor drinks from a glass, which is then picked up by the clone.

1 Put your camera on a tripod, and lock it into position. Use sand bags to keep it in place, if necessary, as absolutely nothing must move until the end of the scene.

2 Shoot your actor in the first chair, taking a drink and putting the glass back down on the table. The glass should be placed in a 'neutral' space between the two seats, and then your actor should sit for a few moments, as though the glass is being picked up by a second person.

3 Immediately move your actor to the second chair, and shoot again without any delay, before the light changes or anything gets moved. Begin by shooting several seconds where this actor does nothing, because this will fill the space when the 'first' actor is moving. Your actor should then take the glass, drink from it and replace it.

EYELINES

If you feel confident with the split screen technique, you can get the two versions of your actor to talk to each other. When doing this, it can help to sit another actor - a double - in the second seat, to give reactions, feed lines and help with timing. Make sure the double is the same height, and sitting in the same position that your actor will sit in, so that your virtual twins appear to be looking into each other's eyes as they talk.

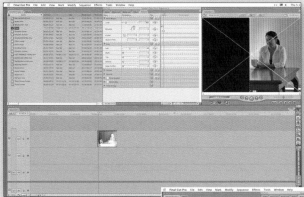

4 Load the footage into your editing package and open the first clip. Using the *Crop* tool, remove the half of the screen with the empty chair but leave the glass in shot. Click the *Keyframe* button.

6 Put the clips together in the *Timeline*, with the cropped clip on the higher layer. Where it has been cut away, the clip below will be revealed. Position the clips so that when the glass has been put down, there is a moment before it is picked up.

5 After the glass is replaced, move the *Crop mark* over to the right, until it is on the right-hand side of the glass. When the clips are combined, this will leave the first shot of the glass visible, until it is about to be picked up from the second position.

7 If you've done everything correctly, you should see the two versions of your actor, passing a drink from one to the other. In most cases you don't need to feather the edges of the crop to make it invisible, but if the join shows up, use a small amount of feathering to hide the line.

160 How to Create a Trombone Shot

You can help an audience share the character's sense of shock by using a trombone shot. During this shot the background appears to change size dramatically, although the actor remains the same size. It's a whooshing, zooming feeling that distorts reality for a moment. The technique was made famous in *Jaws*, when Roy Scheider's character sees a shark attack from the beach. Now used largely for comedic purposes, it is an unmistakably powerful effect.

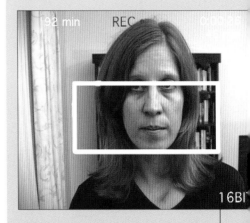

3 Now move very close to your character, and zoom back from your actor to a wider lens, until you've repositioned the nose and chin on the guideframe.

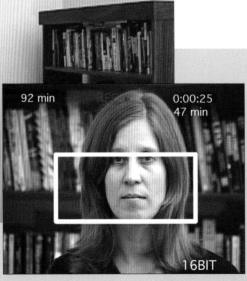

1 Position your actor at least two metres from a distinctive background. If your background is featureless, the effect won't be visible, and if your actor is too close to the background, the result will be minimized.

2 Place the camera about ten feet from the actor, and zoom in so that your actor's nose and chin rest on the white guidelines in your viewfinder. No matter where you move the camera during the shot, or how you change the lens, you should always aim to keep the actor's eyes and chin in the same part of the screen.

4 This will be the finishing point for your shot, so mark the floor so it will be easier for you to hit your mark. If you're using a dolly, mark the position where the dolly should stop.

5 If your camera is on a dolly it will be easy to move, but a handheld approach gives you a real feel for the use of the zoom lens, and can actually make it easier to make the correct adjustments. If your camera is good enough to maintain autofocus, that's the ideal approach, but you can get an assistant to change the focus as you adjust the zoom.

6 Go back to your starting position, zoom in to the correct size and begin the shot. Your actor can look into camera, or just slightly behind camera. As you move forwards, keep zooming out smoothly.

7 Continue zooming out as you move forwards, keeping your actor exactly the same size in frame. The only thing that should change is the background, which will widen, creating an eerie sense of space around your actor. You'll notice that the actor's face also distorts when you're close with a wide lens.

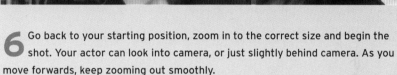

FINISHING TOUCHES

The trombone shot is almost always used when a character realizes something amazing, or sees something shocking. It is usually accompanied by a sound, such as a screeching violin, that reflects the distortion. Don't cut away from this shot until the camera has come to a halt, or the cut may feel too harsh. A trombone shot should be over in about two to three seconds.

How to Shoot Reflections

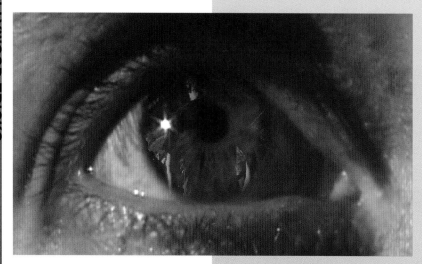

2 Mirror shots work well in wide-screen, or when zoomed in tight on the actors. You don't need to show the whole room, only the frame of the mirror. Actors often give better performances when they know they are both on screen at the same time.

Watch any film by Steven Spielberg and you'll be impressed by how many times he uses mirrors and reflections. A mirror lets you see in two directions at once, so you can see both actors' faces at the same time. This is smoother than always cutting from one actor to the next. Reflections in windows can also be used to create a sense of location. For the ambitious, reflections in an eyeball can create a real moment of drama.

1 A good mirror shot gives some indication of the room your characters are standing in. If the opposing walls are different colours, the effect will be more striking.

3 Avoid going in so tight that you can't tell the mirror is there. If you do, the result looks like one character is standing behind the other, and they appear to be talking to people who aren't there.

4 If you want to show the landscape your actor is looking at without making a cut, shoot an indoor scene as though you are shooting through a window. Give the actor something to lean on to create the impression of a window ledge.

5 Shoot an outdoor location, and add this as a semi-transparent layer in your editing software by reducing the *Opacity* to 50 per cent. This technique is especially powerful for showing somebody arriving at a house. We get to see the arrival and the main character's reaction at the same moment.

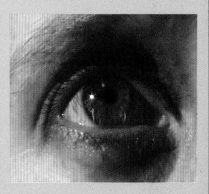

7 You can create this shot in most editing packages, but you'll find it easier in an effects package like Adobe After Effects. Shrink the reflection to fit the iris, and then draw a matte around the iris with the *Pen* tool. Feather the matte by about 4 pixels.

8 The *Composite Mode* should be changed to *Lighten*, and you can add a *Bulge* or *Warp* filter to make the reflection curve slightly, so that it appears to hug the shape of the eyeball. This helps to blend your composite together.

6 To create a reflection in an eyeball, film the eye as close as you can without creating shadows. Take care – if you get too close, the camera's reflection may show up in the pupil. Shoot the footage that you want to appear in the reflection.

REVELATION

Mirrors work best when they show part of the scene without drawing attention to themselves. You can, however, use mirrors for sudden revelations. Your character may be standing next to a mirror when an enemy bursts through the door, showing simultaneous action and reaction. A short lens work best, because it helps keep everything in focus. If you use a long lens, you'll need to change the focus at the moment of revelation.

How to Create a Ghost

Ghosts are quite easy to create, but they are usually more frightening when you can only just see them. This technique makes a semi-transparent ghost appear from nowhere, surrounded by a cloud of glowing light. You can change the level of transparency, colour and glow to suit your film.

1 Shoot the location with your camera on a tripod. Put your actor in place first, to ensure that your camera is correctly set up. Light the scene in a way that leaves a dark or dim space where the ghost will appear.

2 Now shoot your actor as the ghost. Make sure there is plenty of light on the actor, and don't worry that the lighting is different to the master shot. Make sure the camera doesn't move from its original position.

ATMOSPHERE

It is always a good idea to have your main character sense that a ghost is about to appear, or at least be frightened. Music and sound effects will also help to make the ghost seem realistic, as will your main character's reaction when the ghost appears. Although you may be tempted to make the ghost fully visible, the image is more chilling when you can only just see the ghost.

3 In your editing software (here we're using Final Cut Express), place the location shot on a layer beneath the ghost shot in the timeline. Apply a garbage matte around the ghost, then adjust the *Smoothness* and *Feather* sliders so that the ghost blends into the scene gradually.

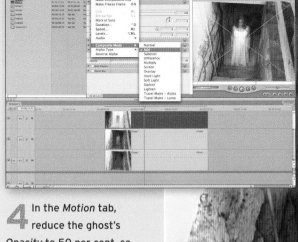

4 In the *Motion* tab, reduce the ghost's *Opacity* to 50 per cent, so you can see through to the layer below. Now duplicate the ghost layer, and place this new layer above the other two. Change its *Composite Mode* to *Add*, and apply a *Zoom Blur* to the layer. This creates the glowing cloud effect.

5 You may need to use the *Color Correction* filters to adjust the ghost layers, so that they blend in with the original shot, although some slight contrast in colour can actually be quite effective.

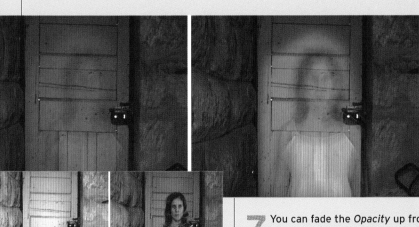

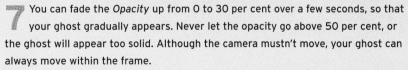

7 You can fade the *Opacity* up from 0 to 30 per cent over a few seconds, so that your ghost gradually appears. Never let the opacity go above 50 per cent, or the ghost will appear too solid. Although the camera mustn't move, your ghost can always move within the frame.

6 For a more dramatic effect you might want to see right through the ghost, so this time shoot a background that is well-lit and clearly visible.

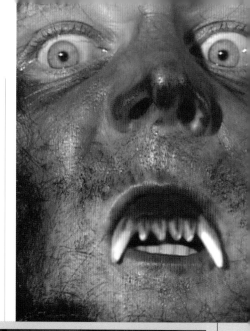
HOLLYWOOD TRICKS

How to Create a Werewolf

Audiences love watching humans turn into werewolves. Although you could cut to another scene while your character transforms, people love to see the change from normal to monster. A simple combination of make-up and editing will give you the results you need. Although horror often works best when it's subtle and barely seen, transformations are dramatic and can be shown in good light, with every detail visible.

1 Always set the scene first, by showing your character in the human state, trying to fight off the transformation. There is more drama to be had in watching the character hold off the change, than in the change itself. You can apply a mist of water, to simulate sweat on the face.

2 Purchase werewolf make-up from a costume outlet, or use ordinary make-up, with black hair from a mohair jumper. Attach the hair with latex glue, available from theatrical make-up suppliers. As each layer goes on, film your actor in exactly the same place, going through the whole transformation routine. This makes editing easier later on.

3 Add the teeth about halfway through the process. When you come to edit the sequence, find two clips that match well in terms of movement, edit them together, then apply a cross-dissolve transition to the edit. This will make the teeth appear to grow into place in less than a second.

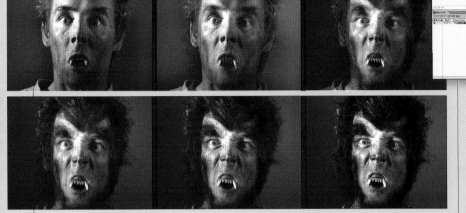

4 The same technique is used for the main transformation. Cut together shots of the different make-up stages, and use a cross dissolve to blend the shots together. Make sure the two shots you are joining match up exactly.

5 When the basic effect is complete, distort the face further by morphing the features. After Effects is one of the best professional programs, but shareware morphing programs can be found on the Web and these give similar results. Drag on the mesh lines to misshape the face. To make the face change shape over time, drag the mesh into a slightly different place at the end of the clip.

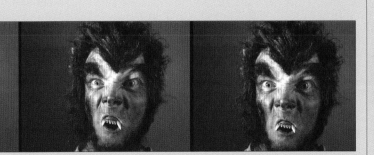

6 With care, your morphing work will make the flesh ripple as though bones and muscles are moving under the skin. Keep the effect small if you want it to look realistic.

7 For a final close-up, you can give the actor yellow contact lenses. If you prefer to do this in the computer, choose the *Change Color* or *Color Correction* filter, select the blue of the eyes, and then shift the *Hue* slider until the eyes turn yellow.

SOUND EFFECTS

Without good sound effects your visuals will be wasted. Record the sound of creaking wood, and slow it down in your audio or video-editing software. Match each creak to a change of expression or moment of transformation. Sound effects can make ordinary shots appear supernatural. Shoot your actor's fingers flexing, then add a creaking sound, and the audience will believe that the hands are transforming painfully.

168 How to Create Small and Tall People

There are several ways of creating people of unusual height. The traditional approach is to create the illusion in the camera, without any software or postproduction. This trick is called 'Forced Perspective' and, with care, it can look better than any computer work. If you want more control over the finished look, however, you might want to use a blue screen to composite your small and tall people together.

2 Place the camera at ground level, and set up the shot so your actors' feet appear to be level with each other. This creates the illusion that they are standing in the same area. They should not look at each other, but should stare into the space next to themselves as though the other person was there, to create the impression of eye contact. Use a long lens, and do not move the camera during the shot.

1 Position your actors on a piece of level ground, some distance apart. It will take experimentation to find the right distance and position.

3 Forced perspective works well when combined with other techniques. The most simple technique of all is to have one actor go down on their knees while the other stands up. This may not look convincing, but works when cut in to other effect shots.

4 To create a more convincing illusion, you'll need to shoot one actor on location, and the other in front of a bluescreen. You'll need a huge bluescreen for this, so you can try using a blue wall, or hanging up a blue sheet. Make sure you put blue paper on the floor, or the actor's feet won't show in the finished shot.

5 Your editing software lets you key the bluescreen away. Shadows may remain around the actor's feet. If so, leave them there, as they help to add realism to the finished shot.

6 Your finished shot will allow you to move one actor behind another. If you want them to look at each other, get each actor to stare into the space where the other would be, and make fine adjustments by shifting the layers around until the result looks right to you.

POINT OF VIEW

For close-ups, shoot each actor from the other's point of view. To shoot the tall actor, put the camera low and angle it upwards. To shoot the small person, put the camera high on your tripod and point it downwards. When you cut between these two shots, this point of view will reinforce the sense of scale.

How to Create Rain

Real rain doesn't show up on camera, because the drops are too small. Rain-machines creates rain that is visible, and while that might be relatively unrealistic, that's all that seems to matter. So long as your rain shows up, nobody minds if it looks brighter and thicker than the real thing. The simplest rain machine is a garden hose with your thumb over the end. When lit correctly, this looks as good as any movie rain. Just make sure you keep the water away from any electric cables.

1 Watch a few movie scenes, and see how rain is often shown pouring down windows in huge rivers. This never happens in the real world, but looks great on screen. Aim a hose at the top of the window, and use a long lens so that the background scenery blurs.

2 Use a *Color Correction* filter in your editing software to add a blue cast to the footage. This helps create the mood of a rainy day.

3 Shoot close-ups of water raining into puddles from a garden watering can. These close-ups can be used to set the scene, or to reinforce the idea that it is raining. Combine this with sound effects, such as thunder.

4 For raindrops to show up you need to spray water between the camera and a light source. Make sure light is shining through the rain, towards the camera. Spray water high in the air, so that your shot only contains the falling droplets, and none that are going upwards.

5 The best results come from combining techniques. Shoot a scene with backlit rain, and shoot water falling from a hose, and combine the shots in the computer. This ensures there is plenty of bright rain in the background and foreground.

6 To create rain during a car scene, first shoot night-time city footage out of a car window. Then, at night, place a projection screen some distance away from your parked car, and project your moving city footage onto the screen. Now spray the front and side of the car with the hose, and film from the opposite side, through the open window. This is a time-consuming setup, but the results are very convincing

7 Cut-aways of wet roads, inserted into the footage, will help to perfect the illusion, but keep these brief, as the rain itself won't show up in these shots.

BACKLIGHT

Rain is only visible when light shines through it, towards the camera. The difficulty with this approach is keeping the lamp itself out of the shoot. The standard trick in Hollywood is to raise the light as high as possible. This way it still shines towards the camera, but is too high to show up in the shot. Don't be tempted to light the rain from the side. Although this may look good to your eyes, it won't show up well in camera.

How to Recreate Absent Props

Police car, fire, computer screen light – all of these things are better simulated than filmed in real life. Shooting televisions is another example. Apart from the copyright issues that broadcast television presents, the shutter speed has to be adjusted for the CRT's scan rate, and this affects the amount of light you will need to illuminate your shot.

In fact, televisions don't throw out the amount or kind of moving light that Hollywood would have us believe. That's because they don't use televisions – they mimic the effect instead. And that's exactly how you do it.

Everyone knows what a television is and how it subtly alters the light in a room. In Hollywood language, it throws out blue flickering light. You can fake this using lighting, but unless you use a 'daylight' halogen lamp you'll need to use a blue gel to get the right colour. Steer away from very dark blues unless you have a very bright light source.

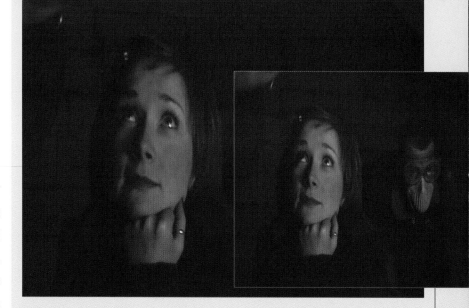

1 In the case of this horror movie, we have our killer hiding in the darkness. That means it needs to be dark enough to keep him in the shadows, then light enough to suddenly reveal him in the glow from the television.

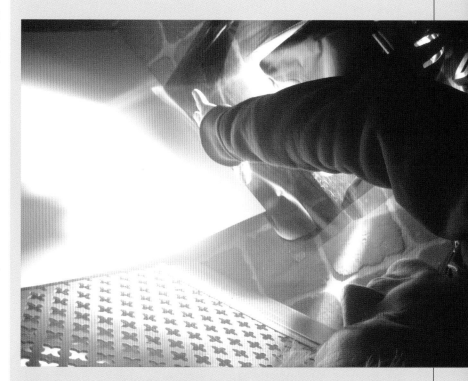

2 Here we're using a standard 'redhead' lamp. The problem with a redhead is that it's exactly that, and just adding a sky blue gel for this shot wasn't strong enough to make the flickering blue light needed. Adding another mid-blue to it worked to get the right shade of believable blue.

3 This redhead and a tight location created another problem. The strong light source was simply too strong, even with the barn doors closed. To ease the strength, the light is aimed away from the subject onto a deflector – just a piece of white card stock.

5 ...and this is how the final video image looks. The killer revealed and the terrified face in close-up – time to cut to the scream!!!!!

4 The final touch to the illusion is an operator simply finding the right-hand movements and speeds to wave in front of the light to mimic movement of lights and darks on the television screen. In front of the lamp, these movements become exaggerated and reflect onto the card stock and back onto the subject's face.

EMERGENCY

You can use exactly the same method for fire – just use a dark orange filter instead. And instead of faking a disturbance on set and dialling the authorities, a well-timed sweep past a dark blue gel onto a reflector will convince any viewer that the police or paramedics are on their way...

How to Shoot Day for Night

Shooting at night is difficult, unless you have lots of portable lighting, and even then the process is time-consuming. If you can avoid dragging your cast and crew into the night air, your production will run more smoothly. By shooting in the day and simulating a night-time look in the camera, you save yourself many headaches. Although the finished results don't look like real night, neither do shots taken during the night and artificially lit. Audiences will accept that it's night time when you shoot day for night.

1 Set up your camera so that there's no sky in the shot. Even cloudy sky will look like daylight, so keep it out of frame by raising your camera a few feet, or shooting where the sky is hidden by the landscape. When color-corrected towards blue your scene will appear to be moonlit.

3 With your footage imported into your software, apply a *Color Correction* filter. You may be tempted to darken the highlights, but the most important change is to shift the hue towards blue, and to destaturate the image slightly.

2 Although harsh sunlight isn't ideal, don't make the mistake of underexposing or shooting everything in shadow. Watch day for night scenes in motion pictures, and you'll see that they're brightly lit. Shoot your actor with normal exposure and colour.

4 The result is not completely realistic, but so long as a sunny sky doesn't stray into your shot, the audience will accept that this is night-time, and that the shadows are made by moonlight.

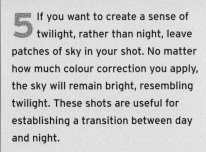

5 If you want to create a sense of twilight, rather than night, leave patches of sky in your shot. No matter how much colour correction you apply, the sky will remain bright, resembling twilight. These shots are useful for establishing a transition between day and night.

6 Night-time car scenes can be shot in an enclosed garage, to resemble night. This gives you more control of lighting than you would have outdoors at night, and your crew remain undercover, so this is a good option during bad weather. Make sure you block off all sources of natural light. As always, do the colour correction when editing, rather than using in-camera effects.

NIGHT EFFECTS

You can enhance all your night-time shots with cutaways. The standard approach is to show a shot of the moon, before cutting to your night-time scene. You can also shoot night-time exteriors, without the need for a full crew, which help to establish the illusion of night. Make sure your actors talk in slightly more hushed tones during day for night shots, as people tend to talk more quietly when they are in dark places.

7 If you want to shoot an indoor scene that's set at night, don't wait until evening. Block off all the exterior light (which would show as blue), and shoot with lots of artificial light. This creates the impression of a night-time indoor scene.

176 How to Build Lunar Landscapes

Landscape mattes are a cost-effective way to create alien landscapes. It takes less than an hour to create a stunning backdrop for your space battle. You can shoot this scene from many angles, to create original landscapes. Almost a hundred years old, this technique is still popular with feature film directors, because it provides incredible realism for a small effort.

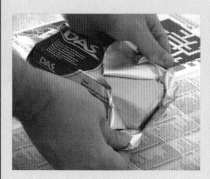

1 Tape the edges of a sheet of newspaper onto your work surface, so that it won't move while you model. Use an air-drying clay, such as Das, which is perfect for creating a moon-like surface.

2 Create a mountain by smearing the edges of the clay down to the newspaper. Although you should make sure that fingerprints aren't visible by the end, the rough impressions left by your finger edges contribute to the look of real rock

3 Roll a ball of clay into a snakelike tube, and use this to make a circle. Smear the edges of this circle and you have a crater. Real craters usually have a small mound at the very centre as well, so you can add a blob of clay to the middle.

4 You don't need to wait for the clay to dry. Sprinkle flour over the model to fill the gaps, adding a rough, gravel-like appearance. Use plenty of flour to cover the newsprint. Use less on the mountains, and make sure you don't add so much flour that everything becomes rounded off. You want to leave some cragginess.

5 Spray the model with grey aerosol paint. Hold the can a good distance from the model, so that the paint falls evenly, without creating dark patches. If you spray from one direction only this will help to emphasize the 3D appearance of your landscape when it is filmed.

6 Check the model for fingerprints, or for chunks of clay that stick up unrealistically. Remember that you will be putting the camera quite close to the model.

7 If you've built a bluescreen, place it behind your model, or just tape a sheet of blue paper to the wall. Shine a strong light source from the side of your model, at about the same height as your work surface, to create strong shadows. Shoot with a short lens, close to the model. When you load the shot into your computer, the blue can be removed with a *Chromakey* or *Bluescreen* filter.

SCENERY

Landscape mattes can be used as scenery for a ship to fly over, or as a background for actors. If you use actors, make sure they are lit in the same way as the landscape matte (with hard light, from a low, sideways direction.) Also, blur the landscape slightly, leaving the actors in focus, to simulate depth.

178 How to Create Space and Stars

Stars may be tiny, but they are an important detail in space-based effects work. Without them, your shot will look incomplete. You can go a step further and create super-nova clouds and rushing lights, to add more of a science-fiction feel. Stars are easy to create, with nothing more than a bag of flour, a straw and black paper.

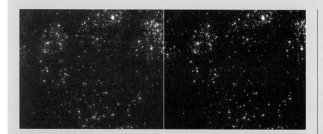

3 Film the paper from directly above. Try to ensure that it is lit from as high an angle as possible, to avoid it shining. Load the shot into your editing software, and adjust the *Contrast* until the black area becomes as dark as space and the white spots look like stars.

1 Tape a large piece of black paper or card onto a level work surface. Make sure there are no wrinkles in the paper.

2 Use a straw to lightly sprinkle flour onto the paper or card. Don't put the straw too close to the paper, or you'll make large blobs. Flick the end of the straw with your finger to make the flour splash out.

4 Add your landscape matte over this layer, and your lunar location is complete. Stars don't need to move or twinkle, because in space stars appear to be stationary, and don't flicker.

TWINKLE

If you want your stars to twinkle, as though they are being seen through an atmosphere, you'll need a different approach. Attach your black paper to a wall, then stick tiny pieces of silver foil to strands of thread, and suspend them in front of the paper. Film the result while blowing on the thread to make the stars glitter. You only need a handful of twinkling stars, placed over your star background, to give the impression that they are all twinkling.

5 To create a supernova, drop a large blob of flour on the sheet and then blow through the straw, so that the flour spreads out, leaving a dark hole at the centre. Add this layer to your footage, using the *Add Composite* mode.

6 To create the illusion of space dust or an ion cloud, sprinkle the paper quite heavily with flour, and apply a *Motion Blur* filter to the layer.

7 To create a three-dimensional space cloud, shoot another flour pattern, then load it into your editing software. This time, use *Color Correction* to shift its colour towards red. Apply a *Radial Blur* filter, to spread the light upwards.

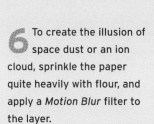

How to Shoot Miniatures

A small model spaceship can easily look like a gigantic battle cruiser, when blended into your movie. By raising your model in front of a bluescreen, you can move your camera around the miniature, which makes it look as though the model is flying. This is far more practical than flying your model around on strings, and it creates the most brilliant, swooping shots.

1 Attach your model to a short pole, painted with the same paint you used for your bluescreen. You can use modelling clay or Blu-tack to secure the support pole. Arrange your bluescreen so that it sits behind the model, but don't let hard shadows from the model fall on the screen's surface. Make sure that the blue pole never shows in front of the ship, or that part of the ship will vanish when the filter is applied.

2 Using the *Bluescreen* or *Chromakey* filter, remove the blue screen, and feather the edges of your image, so that the ship appears to exist above your landscape and stars.

3 By colour correcting all the layers, you can make them appear as if they are lit by the same light source.

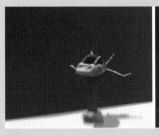   

4 To make the ship move, leave it exactly where it is, but 'fly' your camera towards and around the model. Handheld camerawork is fine, and if you move quite quickly you'll add realistic motion blur. Never let any part of the ship overlap the edge of the blue screen (as seen through the camera), or you won't be able to use the shot.

5 You don't need to move your background stars for this shot to work. Simply use your application's *Bluescreen* or *Chromakey* filter to remove the bluescreen, and the result will look realistic.

6 To create a fleet of ships, just shoot your model from a variety of angles, moving in a number of directions. Be careful not to change the model's position or lighting, or you will make the finished shot look jumbled and confused.

HARD LIGHT

If your spaceship is meant to be in space, lit by a sun, you should use one strong lamp to light your model. Don't add any filters to soften the light, because in space harsh sunlight produces hard shadows. If your spaceship will be flying through an atmosphere, you can bounce the light off a wall to create softer shadows.

7 Load all the different shots into your computer, and layer them on top of each other. Shrink the models to different sizes with the *Scale* slider or a similar tool, and drag the layers to different positions on screen.

How to Create an Explosion

You can create stunning movie explosions without ever putting yourself in danger, for almost no cost. Water balloons, when lit from behind, create the illusion of exploding fire. This technique has been used in film and TV for years, because it is simple and cost-effective. Water balloons explode in a convincing way, and when lit with a tungsten light, the blast looks like fire.

1 Suspend a water-filled balloon in front of a bluescreen, or in a dark room. Arrange your lamp so that light comes towards the camera and through the balloon. This will make the water glow.

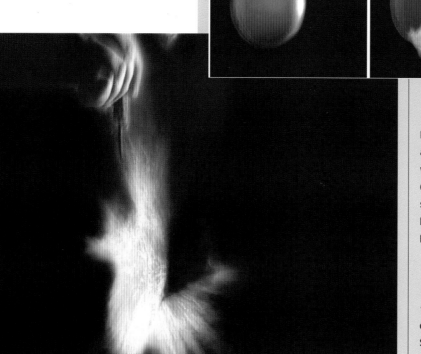

2 Keep the camera a good distance from the balloon, and zoom in. This keeps water off your lens. Roll camera and pop the balloon by a thread. If you want to keep your hands out of shot (for easier compositing later), you can suspend the balloon with cotton and burst it by holding a portable gas burner nearby until the rubber melts.

3 The explosion will be very rapid, so set the shutter rate of your camera to a high speed (such as the Sports/Action setting) to capture the full effect.

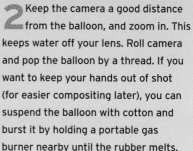

4 A mixture of half air and half water will give you good results, but experiment with different sizes of balloon and amounts of water. For a really bloated explosion, use lots of water. For a more gaseous explosion, more air is better.

6 In your editing software, add the water explosion and sparkler frames on top of your background footage. Change the *Composite Mode* of these layers to *Add*, and then drag the layers until the explosion is in the correct place. You can also draw a garbage matte around the footage, to take away the sharp edges.

5 Get hold of some hand-held sparklers (from a novelty store or firework distributor), and light one in a darkened room. Film the sparkler from several distances. Moving sparkler footage doesn't work well, but when you insert a couple of still frames of sparkler footage into the water explosion, they add to the bursting effect.

MOVING FOOTAGE

If your spaceship moves across the screen, the explosion should move at the same rate. Go to the beginning of the shot, and position the explosion layer in the correct place, and select the *Motion* tab. Click the *Position Keyframe* button to record the layer's current position. Now go to the end of the clip and drag the explosion layer into the new position, so they appear to have moved with the spaceship. The computer should automatically match the layers throughout the entire shot.

7 The finished result will be over in less than a second. Make sure you fade out the water clip after just a few frames, or the effect of water being pulled down by gravity will give the game away.

Glossary

16:9 The widescreen ratio used by widescreen televisions, projectors and some digital video cameras.

24p Digital video shot or shown at 24 frames per second, in progressive scan mode. This results in a more 'film-like' moving image.

4:3 The standard screen ratio of non-widescreen televisions and early Hollywood films. Sometimes referred to as 1.33:1.

ADR (Additional Dialogue Recording) Re-recorded dialogue, added to the audio mix in the studio to assist cutting, resolve narrative issues or solve audio flaws.

Anamorphic The process of squeezing a widescreen image at capture, so that it fits onto a frame of film or a CCD, then stretching it out during playback so that it fits within a 16:9 ratio.

Artifacts A visual disturbance of an image caused by flaws in the image-capture or storage systems.

Atmos (Atmosphere) The ambient audio that already exists on a set or in a location.

Barndoors Four metal hinged doors fixed to the rim of a lamp, which can be moved in and out of the light's direction to vary the level and intensity of the light.

Batch Capture Automated capture of a tape's images using a log of clips to capture and the timecode embedded in the tape.

Bitrate The quantity of data in a stream of digital data, measured in terms of how many bits (digital 1s and Os) go through the stream each second (bits or kilobits per second). As a rule in video, the higher the bitrate, the higher the quality of the audio or video, but the more demands placed on whatever carries, processes or stores the data.

Broadcast Legal The strict (but loosening) code of practice that only permits certain chrominance and luminance values in a video signal. This helps maintain the quality and consistency of broadcast TV signals across the full variety of TV sets.

Capture The process of a computer storing the important video and audio data from an input source, usually a digital video camera.

Cardioid The heart-shaped pattern of audio sensitivity around a microphone. This can also be super or hypercardioid, which narrows the shape and extends the range.

CPU (Central Processing Unit) The main chip inside a computer, responsible for processing all of its active operations and running any applications.

CCD (Charge-Coupled Device) The light sensitive chip inside a DV camera, which transforms beams of light coming through the lens into a series of electrical signals.

Chrominance The colour values of an image, measured in RGB levels.

Claw Ball The ball at the head of a tripod that allows for levelling the camera or rotating it in multiple axes.

Close-Up A shot that shows a detail of a subject or object.

Condenser A microphone that uses a sensitive, electrically charged diaphragm to pick up sound.

Coverage The amount of shots filmed to grab enough footage to create a scene.

Cut The end of one shot or scene and the beginning of the next without a transition.

Cutaway An interposing shot placed between two shots to convey information or cover and blend an awkward moment.

Db (Decibel) A unit measure that expresses audio changes in signal or power.

Deflector Reflectors used to redirect light to a particular part of the scene or frame.

De-Interlace The isolation and combination of the upper or lower interlaced field of a frame captured on standard digital video to create a distinct image or simulate the effect of progressive scan.

Depth of Field A measurement of the range in front of the lens in which objects in an image will appear in clear focus.

Dialogue Fictional conversation between two or more subjects.

Digital8 A Sony digital video format, which uses the 8mm tape employed in the old Hi-8 analogue standard to store DV data. While inexpensive and backwards compatible, the quality isn't usually as good as MiniDV.

Dissolve An audio/video transition that mixes two shots through the lowering of opacity on the first with a simultaneous raising of opacity on the second.

Dolly A small vehicle running along tracks. It supports the camera, ensuring smooth camera movements that follow the action around the set or landscape.

Drop Frame The process by which NTSC rectifies 29.97 frames per second by dropping two frames every minute, with the exception of every tenth minute.

DTV (Digital Television) An umbrella term that incorporates digital broadcast in SDTV and HDTV formats.

Dubbing The revoicing of lines of dialogue in an audio edit.

Dynamic Range The audio measure between the softest and loudest levels of a signal.

EDL (Edit Decision List) A list of timecodes, covering every *In* and *Out* point of every clip on the *Timeline*.

Encoder A program that converts digital data from one format into the digital data required for another format, for example, converting DV video to MPEG-2 for DVD.

EQ (Equalizer) A facility that allows for the amplification or softening of particular frequencies in an audio signal.

Establisher A shot that establishes the location of the scene.

Exposure The amount of light that is permitted to enter the camera via the lens, as dictated by the aperture.

Extra An actor who takes a background, non-speaking role within a scene.

Extreme Close-Up A tight close-up framed to exaggerate a detail.

Eyelight A light placed to add twinkle or shine to a subject's eyes.

Fade A decrease of opacity towards the end of the shot, usually fading to black.

Field One of the two parts of an image (upper or lower) that a television signal interlaces to create an illusion of the complete frame.

FireWire The Apple-coined term for the IEEE-1394 interface standard, as used by most DV cameras and capture cards.

Foley The recreation of sound effects for recording as part of the audio track.

Frequency The number of cycles per second of an audio waveform, measured in Hertz (Hz).

Gain An electronic circuit that amplifies a video or audio signal.

Gate A facility in an audio edit that limits the volume of an audio signal to a designated level.

Gel Acetates used in front of a light that either compensates for a colour imbalance or adds a particular colour cast to the scene.

Gobo An inverse shape fixed to a light designed to cast light and shadow in the inverse of that shape.

Grading A post-production term for the overall look given by the crominance and luminance values of an image. These days, whole scenes or films can be graded digitally to achieve a particular effect.

Halogen A lamp with a light temperature close to that of daylight.

Hi-8 An analogue video format similar to S-VHS, but using 8mm tape.

HDTV (High Definition Television) A new standard for the recording and displaying of images, with close to double the resolution of SDTV.

Hot-Plugging Adding or removing hardware whilst the computer is fully operating, with the computer and the device communicating instantly and on-demand.

Hue The shade of colour attributed to a pixel or an entire image.

IEEE-1394 A connection that allows data transfer of up to 800Mbps and the standard interface between DV cameras and computers.

iLink Sony's term for IEEE-1394.

Interlacing The process whereby a conventional CRT television produces an image from two frames, one comprising the odd horizontal lines and one comprising the even horizontal lines, alternating between them at 60 frames per second to create the illusion of a single image updating at 30 frames per second.

Jaggies A stair-like line within an image, usually caused a by lack of resolution. Jaggies are smoothed away by antialiasing.

Jump-Cut A deliberately unsettling cut in an edit that joins two shots in a way that breaks traditional Hollywood conventions. For example, the shots may be too similar or the change might be very abrupt.

Keyframe A concept borrowed from traditional animation, where a lead artist would draw the most important frames of a sequence and junior artists would then create the inbetween frames. In digital

Glossary

video, keyframes are used to control an effect or animation. The user sets a keyframe and alters the values of parameters or the position of an element, then sets another keyframe for the next change. The computer will then calculate the effects on the frames in-between.

Keying A process where a video-editing or effects package selects an area of screen based on either chrominance (Chromakey) or luminance (Luma Key), which the computer will replace with another image.

Lock-Off A camera firmly mounted in place on a tripod for the duration of a static shot.

Long Shot A shot that frames the entirety of a subject in their surroundings.

Luminance The amount of light attributed to a pixel or image.

Master Shot One extended shot that covers the whole of a scene, sequence or event, incorporating all the dialogue and action.

Matte A digital mask that defines the area of transparency for compositing or keying.

Medium Shot A shot that frames the subject from slightly above the waist to the top of the head.

MicroMV Sony's digital format that uses MPEG-2 compression to copy video to a tape smaller than Mini-DV cassettes.

MiniDV Standard consumer digital video format, which records to 1/4 inch tape.

Mise-en-scene The deliberate composition of elements (actors, colours, props, set-design) in a scene.

MPEG-2 File compression standard for digital video, principally for use by the DVD format, and set by the Motion Pictures Expert Group.

MPEG-4 File compression standard set by the Motion Pictures Expert Group, aimed at the distribution of video across the Internet.

NLE (Non-linear Edit) A digital editing system, which allows a movie to be assembled in any order, so that shots can be shuffled or repositioned and effects or transitions added at will, without needing to work through the film sequentially. Non-linear editing is a more flexible and intuitive process than traditional film editing or linear video editing.

Opacity A percentage attribute given to a video clip to control its level of transparency.

Pan A camera movement along the horizontal axis or an audio movement from the left to right or right to left speaker.

Plug-in A small, separate program which 'plugs-in' to a larger application in order to extend or improve its features.

Post-Roll During a batch capture, the amount of time a tape continues to be captured after the *Out* point is reached.

POV (Point Of View) A camera shot undertaken at a character's eye-level and understood as being from their perspective.

Practical An on-set light that is part of the set dressing and operates in the frame.

Pre-Roll During a batch capture, the amount of time a tape pre-captures before the *In* point is reached.

Progressive Scan A way of refreshing a television screen or other display without interlacing. The image is displayed in one frame, running continually line after line at 30 frames per second for a smoother, flicker-free display.

Rack Focus Changing focus between two parts of the frame through a change in the depth of focus.

Redhead A small, powerful and portable Halogen light.

Reflector A board with a reflective surface, used to reflect and soften light onto a set.

Safety Take A further take of a shot undertaken to ensure that there is something safe and in the can.

Sample Rate The amount of times per second an the audio or video signal is sampled. The higher the sample rate, the closer the sample to the original signal, and so the higher the quality.

Saturation The strength of colour in a colour video signal.

Scratch Disk Disk drive or disk space allocated as a quick-access cache for capturing and previewing clips.

Script A blueprint of the narrative broken down into separate lines of dialogue and short visual directions.

Set An area of a location or stage that will be used in-frame for a scene in a movie.

Setup A shot of a scene, with all the elements of the movie (the camera, the actors, audio, the set) tailored to match.

Shoot Ratio The ratio describing the amount of footage that is shot on set to the amount that is actually used in the master edit.

Shooting Schedule A diary breakdown of all crew, talent, setups and locations required to undertake a day's shoot.

Shooting Script A script that has been finalised artistically and technically, ready for production.

Shutter Speed The number of frames per second that are sampled from the CCD.

Slowmo Running a clip at less than 100% speed in the edit in order to slow the clip down and give a slow-motion effect.

Sound Check A quick rehearsal prior to the shoot to gauge the levels of audio for correct recording.

Sound Effect A sound recorded and imported onto the editing *Timeline* to simulate the sound of something either in or out of the frame.

Storyboard A scene broken down into a series of images to represent the angles, composition and sequence of shots.

Synopsis An abbreviated description of a narrative in prose form.

Take A version of a shot running from 'action' to 'cut'.

Tight A close-in shot with a longer focal length.

Tilt A basic camera movement where the camera pivots on the vertical axis.

Timecode A number given in hours, minutes, seconds and frames for every frame of video, to enable it to be logged for batch capture or editing purposes.

Timeline A single or multitrack line representing the length of video and audio clips during editing in chronological order. Clips can be dragged to the *Timeline*, arranged in order, cut and extended.

Tracking Shot A moving camera shot where the camera itself moves to follow a subject and keep them in frame. The name stems from the Hollywood practice of mounting the camera on tracks to keep this sort of movement smooth.

Transition A change from one shot to another that uses an effect instead of a straight cut, and relating to the compression or decompression of time.

Treatment A commercially viable outline of how the synopsis would be treated as a technical and artistic production.

USB2 A computer interface standard allowing for high-speed data transfer between a PC and a peripheral device. Some DV cameras now come with USB2 connections, but FireWire remains a more popular standard, particularly as it allows for more connection options (camera to camera, camera to digital VCR, and so on).

Video Card An add-in card containing a graphics chip which turns data from a computer's CPU into a video signal that can be shown on a monitor or other display. Not to be confused with a video-capture or video-effects card, which allows video to be digitized from various sources or effects and transitions to be rendered in realtime.

Voice Of God A soundtrack containing narration or voiceover in a movie.

White Balance Information sampled by or given to the camera to establish the median colour temperature of a shot.

Wide A shot covering more of the area around an object, shot with a shorter focal length than average.

Widescreen A screen ratio where the horizontal width is much larger than the vertical height. Widescreen ratios are standard in Hollywood movies. The term has also become used to describe the 16 9 ratio used in modern TV sets.

Wipe A transition that wipes a new clip over an old one.

Zoom The process of moving focal length from a loose, wide-angle shot to a tight, heavily magnified close-up.

Index

A

accessories 20-1
action 40, 58, 76-7, 78, 134, 152
ADC (Analog-to-Digital Converter) 14
ADR (Additional Dialogue Recording) 117
AIFF files 113, 120
AMD Athlon 22
analog-digital comparison 12-13, 14
angles 78, 115
antagonists 76
arcs 34, 36, 38, 41, 76
art department 54-5
artifacts 19, 24, 71
aspect ratio 82
atmos 73, 114, 116, 118, 164
audio 20-1, 24-5, 28-9, 34
    editing 110-25
    final cut 88
    operators 122
    patterns 21
    preproduction 37, 44, 52, 58-9, 72-5
    settings 83
    shooting 58-9, 72-5
    transitions 90
auditions 50
authoring 26, 29, 132
auto-saving 83
AVI files 28, 128-9, 131, 135

B

backlight 171
bandwidth 134
batteries 19-20, 46-7, 58, 79
bi-directions 21
bins 85
bitrates 130-1, 135
black comedy 43
blood 149-51
bluescreen 139, 140-1, 142
blur 66, 99, 121, 177
body language 61
broadband 134
budget 8, 32-3, 44, 46, 48, 54-5, 62,
    138-9, 154
build 76
bulbs 68

C

cables 48, 75, 82, 138, 170
cameras 14-15, 19, 23, 58-9, 82
    capture 84-5
    control 66-7
    editing 82
    moving shots 64-5
    operators 52, 79
capture 84-5
car chases 154-5
cardioid 20, 72
cast 50, 107, 174
CCD (Charge Coupled Device) 12, 14-15, 66, 71
CD-RW drives 25
CDs 25, 28, 128-9
characters 34-9, 41, 43, 50, 55, 76, 90
chargers 19
checklists 58
chromakey 139, 142-3
chrominance 14, 24, 26, 28, 134
claw ball leveller 20
cleaners 28, 131-2, 134
clones 158-9
closing titles 106, 107
codecs (Compress/Decompress) 26, 129
colour
    correction 68, 98, 101-5, 128
    gels 58, 70, 172, 173
    grading 102-4
    temperature 68
comedy 42-3
composition 63
compression 14, 26, 28, 71, 113, 128-30, 134
computers 22-3, 82, 84, 114, 128
contacts 33
continuity 75, 78
contracts 50
copyright 120, 172
costumes 62, 90
CPU (Central Processing Unit) 22
crawls 106
credits 46-8, 107, 132
crew 48, 52-3, 107, 146, 174
CRT (Cathode Ray Tubes) 24, 172
CU (close-ups) 44, 55, 61, 75, 78, 87-8
cutaways 55, 61, 78, 116-17, 139, 175
cutting 78-9, 88-9

D

DAC (Digital-to-Analog Converter) 15
day for night 174-5
DDR SDRAM memory 22
deflectors 71
180-degree rule 74-5
depth of field 13, 66
device control 83
dialogue 72-6, 78, 87, 90, 95, 113-14, 116-18,
    125, 139
diaries 33, 132
Digital8 standard 15
Digital Effects 18
Discreet Cleaner XL 131
dissolve transitions 90-1
distribution 26, 37, 50, 52, 120, 126-35
dogme 13
dollies 65
download speeds 134
drama 38-9
dream sequences 18, 99, 156
drop frame timecodes 83
dubbing audio 122-3
duplicate shots 78
DVDs 22, 25, 28-9, 104, 128-33
DVI (Digital Visual Interface) 24
dynamic range 112, 114

E

echo 99, 121
effects 18-19, 27-8, 36, 73, 139
    final cut 84, 86, 98, 100-1
    night 175
    sound 113, 121, 124-5, 164, 167
EIS (Electronic Image Stabilizers) 19
encoding 14, 26, 28, 131-2, 134
end shots 19
EQs (equalizers) 118-19
establishers 44, 60
explosions 182-3
export 128
exposure 16, 58-9, 66
extras 50
eyelights 70
eyelines 75, 78, 158

F

f-stops 66

fades 90, 92

features 18-19

fees 46

fight scenes 152-3

file formats 113, 120, 128, 131-2, 135

file size 129, 134

filters 72, 98-102, 104, 118-19, 133

Final Cut Express 22

Final Cut Pro 22, 85, 88, 102

fine cuts 84

FireWire 23, 82, 84, 128

flashbacks 44, 99, 156-7

flip-out screens 19

focus 16, 66, 78

footage 84-5, 183

forced perspective 168

frame rate 82-3, 101

frequencies 118-19, 122

fresnels 70

G

gates 72, 122, 124

gels 58, 70, 172, 173

genre 38-9, 62, 78, 125, 138, 150

ghosts 164-5

GHz (Gigahertz) 22

gobos 70

Golden Section 63

graphics 84, 86

greenscreen 139, 141

guerrilla filmmaking 46

gunshots 148-9

gyros 19

H

hard cuts 90

hard light 181

hardware 22, 24-5, 129

HDD (Hard Disk Drive) 22, 82-4, 135

HDTV (High Definition Television) 14

headphones 72-3, 75, 118, 122

Hi-8 tapes 23

hierarchy 52

housekeeping 85, 128

hypercardioid 72

I

i-Link 23

IEEE 1394 23

image stabilizers 19

iMovie 22

importing footage 84-5

In-movie titles 106, 109

incidental music 120, 121

infoLITHIUM batteries 19

inserts 78

Intel Pentium 22

interlaced scan 24

Internet 22, 50, 52, 123, 129, 134-5

J

jaggies 24

jitters 121

jump shots 115

jump-cuts 61

juxtaposition 90

K

Kelvin scale 68

keyboard shortcuts 84

keyframes 124

kickers 70

L

labels 58, 85

landscape mattes 176-7

laughs 42-3

lavaliers 21, 59, 72, 73, 75

LCD (Liquid Crystal Display) 24

leads 50

lenses 16-17, 59, 65, 163

Li-ion (Lithium ion) 19

lighting 16, 28, 37, 48, 52

   final cut 90

   hard 181

   shooting 58-9, 62, 68-71, 75, 78

   tricks 139, 174, 177

location 44, 46-8, 60, 62, 76, 78, 90, 118,139

lock-offs 20

look 12-13

LS (long shots) 60, 78

luminance 14, 24, 26, 28, 134

lunar landscapes 176-7

M

McGuffin 41, 55

Macs 22, 82, 113, 128, 134

magic hour 33

make-up 52, 54-5, 58, 139, 166

master mix 125

master shots 78, 87-8

menu design 132-3

MicroMV cameras 19, 23

mics 20-1, 52, 58, 72-3, 75

   editing 117, 119, 122

   tricks 138

miniatures 180-1

MiniDV 15-16, 19-20, 23, 129

mise-en-scene 62

mixers 28-9, 119

mixing 113, 115, 117, 123-5

modems 134

money-making 6-7

monitors 24, 75

montage 61

mood 37

motherboard 22

MOV files 128, 129

movie language 94-7, 102, 115

moving footage 183

MPEG files 15, 26, 71, 128, 130-1, 134-5

MS (medium shots) 61

multimedia 22

multitakes 77

multitasking 33

music 34, 37, 90, 107, 113-14

   editing 120-3, 125

   tricks 164

N

navigation 84

night effects 175

NiMH (Nickel Metal Hydride) 19

NTSC (National Television Standards Committee) 13-14, 66, 82-3, 128

O

objectives 40

obstacles 40

offbeat comedy 42-3

OIS (Optical Image Stabilizers) 19

Index

old film effects 100-1
omnidirections 21
online movies 134-5
opening titles 106
outtakes 78, 94, 107

P

PAL (Phase Alternation Line) 13-14, 66, 82-3, 128
panning 19-20, 64, 124-5
PCs 22, 25, 82, 85, 113, 128, 134
Photoshop 132-3
Picture Effects 18
pitch shift 121
plots 34-7, 40-3
plug-ins 28, 118
ports 23
postproduction 72, 142
POV (Point of View) shots 65, 75, 77-9, 138, 169
power surges 82
practical music 120-1
pre-postroll 83
priority lists 33
processing power 27
production costs 8
production values 8, 48, 58, 62, 102-3, 138
progressive scan 24
props 48, 54-5, 58, 61-2
    shoot 72, 76, 78
    tricks 139, 172-3
protagonists 76
pull-out 19
punch sounds 153
pushes 18

Q

quick release plates 20
Quicktime 134

R

rain 170-1
RAM (Random Access Memory) 22
razoring 124-5
reaction shots 44, 78, 117
RealMedia 134

recordable CDs 24
recordable DVDs 25
reflections 162-3
reflectors 71
refraction 16
rehearsals 46, 47, 78, 152
release forms 50
rendering 26-7, 113, 116, 128
reputation 47
resolution 14, 24, 26, 85, 132, 134
revelation 163
rewritable CDs 25
rewritable DVDs 25
rolls 106
romance 43
rough cuts 84
rules 85
runners 47, 52
running man icon 66

S

Sample Rate 134
saving work 83
scares 41-2
scene-setting 48-9, 88
schedules 33, 58
scratch disk 83
screen grabs 52
screenplay 36-7
scrims 71
scripts 58, 76, 78, 82, 117
scriptwriting 36-7, 40, 50
sequencers 28-9, 120
servers 134
servo sounds 20
sets 48-9, 52, 62
settings 82-3
setups 78, 119
shocks 41-2
shooting ratio 22, 79
shooting scripts 78
shortcuts 84
shots 44, 46-7, 52, 58, 60-1, 139
    action 76-7
    framing 62-3, 64, 78
    lists 82

master 78, 87, 88
    trombone 160-1
shutter speed 16, 58, 66, 172
slapstick 42
slow motion 99, 121
small people 168-9
smoke 144-5, 146
software 26-9, 114
sound 24-5, 28-9, 34, 37, 44, 58
    cards 24-5
    editing 110-25
    effects 113, 124, 164, 167
    operators 52
    punch 153
    tips 72-5
soundtracks 19, 120-1
space 178-9
spare batteries 19
speakers 24, 125
sponsorship 33, 37
spots 70
stabilizers 58
standby 19
stars 50-1, 178-9
stereo 124, 125
stills 106, 133
stopping down 66
stories 34-5, 37
storyboards 28, 40, 44-5, 55, 62
    distribution 132
    final cut 82
    mode 86-7
    moving 84
    shoot 78
streaming media 26, 28, 129
studs 20
subjects 40
submenus 132
sunspots 16
super cardioid 72
supporting actors 50
suspense 40-1
symbolism 37, 44
sync dialogue 113-14
synopsis 37

T

tall people 168-9

tape 58, 79, 82, 84-5, 128, 129

taste-free 42

telescopes 20

themes 34, 36-7, 42

three-point lighting 68-70

thunder 115

tilt 20, 64-5

time passing 90-2

timecodes 83

timeframe 32-3, 44, 46-8, 58, 62, 138-9

timeline 26, 86-8, 94-7, 112-13

    audio 115-17, 119, 122-3, 125

    distribution 128

titles 84, 86, 132, 206-9

tow trucks 155

tracking shots 65

trail 18

transcoding 131

transitions 62, 64, 84-6, 90-3, 106, 116,
    120-1, 128

transport 46

treatments 37

tricks 136-83

tripods 20, 58, 64-5

trombone shots 160-1

troubleshooting 46

TV screens 24, 82

twinkling stars 178

U

UHF 21

underwater scenes 146-7

V

VCR 84

VHF 21

VHS tapes 23

video capture cards 23-4, 27, 82

voice-overs 72, 113

volume control 72, 114-15, 117, 121, 123

W

walk-ons 50

wardrobe 54-5, 58, 139

water balloons 182-3

WAV files 113, 120

waveforms 112, 123

werewolves 166-7

white balance 58, 68

widescreen 14, 82

Windows 85, 134

Windows Media 134

wipe 92

wounds 150-1

X

XCU (extreme close-ups) 61

Z

zoom 18-19, 64, 121

Acknowledgements

Talent before the camera:
Louise Bartlett
Elisabeth Bayliffe
Peter Darlo
Barrie Dunn
Kathryn Fleet
Jane Lesley
Sean Moody
Parveen Nabi
Jonathan Rice
Clea Smith
Guy Venables
The Fleshpuppets

Talent behind the camera:
Michael Bartlett
NAPA:NEE
www.MakingTheFilm.com
Photographs by Julian Newman Turner

Maxim Jago
Kiss Chase
www.maximjago.com

Will Jewell
www.fracturedfilms.com
www.willjewell.com

Industry Talent
Robin Charney, Matrox
Dan Loshak, Discreet
Kathryn Lamb, KL Associates
Ulead Systems

Thanks to Chris Kenworthy
for technical assistance and
contributions to Chapter 7